I Guess You Had To Be There

By Doug Rasmusson

Cartoons by Delmar Holdgrafer

Cover designed and painted by Avis Brandt

© 1997

All rights reserved. No part of this book may be copied in any form or by any electronic or mechanical means, including information storage and retrieval systems, without written permission from the publisher, except for brief passages quoted in a review.

First edition 1997
Second printing 1998

Library of Congress Card Number 97-94141

ISBN 0-9659896-0-7

Echo Printing. Alexandria, Minnesota

The original printing of this book was funded in part by a grant from the McKnight Foundation through the Lake Region Arts Council.

Published by Asgard Publishing
      P. O. Box 454
      Hancock, Minnesota 56244

Dedication

To my wife Louise, who has patiently corrected my spelling and grammar, encouraged me when needed, and told me forcibly when I was getting out of line.

To Alys Culhane, who motivated me to start writing in the first place, not a small task with an ancient Norwegian.

To Carol Oen who brought books and expertise to our house, and shamed me into working at putting this collection together.

To all the folks who have told me things that I thought needed repeating.

And to Lorraine Thompson and Jill Landwehr who diligently and patiently removed commas, shortened sentences and tried in vain to teach me that "The person who" is more acceptable than "The person that".

About the Author

As no one else has much to say about Doug Rasmusson, I will endeavor to say a little myself. I am a retired farmer, of Norwegian ancestry, a graduate of Concordia College, a Lutheran, married to Louise, the mother of our three children, we have one grandchild and I am somewhat addicted to long, rambling sentences and a few too many commas. And occasionally, in spite of the best efforts of some good, well meaning people who have helped edit and correct, will start a sentence with a conjunction. But if you continue reading in this book, that will all become abundantly clear to you.

Introduction

I have been told that you do not have to know how to spell pinochle in order to play the game, and you do not need to know how an internal combustion engine works in order to drive a car. Therefore, in spite of some difficulties with computers, it was suggested that I should be able to put together a book. This is an attempt to do just that, and if you are reading it, that should indicate I was successful.

These are stories that I have written over the years; many have been in the local papers. They are about local things and local people mostly, as I seldom get far from home. We live equidistant, five miles from Hancock, Morris, and Cyrus on the south end of Long Lake, one of the hundred or so lakes by that name in our state. Louise's roots are in Western North Dakota so we get there occasionally, and into northeastern North Dakota to visit friends and eat lutefisk. Otherwise I may get to Chokio on the west, Benson on the south, north a little further, as far as Fergus Falls sometimes. East is the exception, as we go to Wisconsin occasionally to see our daughter and her husband in Ladysmith.

If you have bought this book, bless you, if you received it as a gift, fine, but if you have borrowed it, shame on you. I've got to sell them or the attic floor will collapse.

Contents

People
I Guess You Had to be There	3
Memorial Day	4
Cliff Olson	5
Esterly	7
Aging Gracefully	8
Transportation	9
Barbra	11
Funerals	11
WeeWee	13
Migrating Like the Falcons	15
Superman	16
Fertilizer	17
Rabbits	18
Belly Buttons	19
Shakespeare	20
Country School	21
Staying in One Place	23
Ross	24
Conception	26
Consideration	27

Weather
Busy, Busy, Busy	31
Dry Winter Air	32
It's Cold	33
The Blizzard of 1996	34
Snow Plowing	35
Big Day	36
Wasting Time	37
What I Hear When I Shut Up	39
Pocket Gophers	40
The Weather	41

Clothing
Fashion "Look"	45
Caps	46
Use It All Up	48
Clothes with a Message	49
Overalls	50
Pants	52

Animals

Wood Ducks	55
Dinosaurs	56
Where are the Meadowlarks?	57
More Birds	58
Even More Birds	59
Fertility	60
Fishing	61
Ducks	62
The Ocean	64

Health

Smells	69
Walking	70
The New Thumb	71
I'm Not Much Good Anymore	72
Guarding One's Health	73
Striving for Good Health	74
Hearing	76
Exercise	77
Interdependence	78
Earwax	79
Old Geezers	80
Geezerhood	81
Cosmetic Surgery	82
Shopping	83
My Head Cold	84

Opinions

The Bridges of Madison County	89
County Roads	90
How to Operate a Computer	91
White Castle	92
The Bell Ringers	94
Traveling	95
Air Bags	96
Center of the World	97
Loss of Appetite	98
Ethnic Food	98
The Best Place to Live	101
Caucuses	102
Barbie	103
Housework	104
Mildly Vulgar	105
Factoid	106

Words We Know But Don't Use Much	108
Neckties	109
Education	110
Nude Dancing	111
Freedom to Farm	112
Finishing Sentences	113
Friendship	114
The Spirit World	115
Bartlett's	116
The Stairway	118

Places

The Biltmore Estate	123
Empty Buildings	124
Advertising	125
The County Fair	127
Our Hope For The Future	128
Medora	129
Thanksgiving	131

Food

Dessert	135
The Diet	136
The Miracle	137
The Pelican	138
Tator Tot Hot Dish	139
A Cultural Event	140
Microwaves	141
August	142

Unclassified

Emotions	145
The Unibomber	146
Adult Entertainment	147
Comets	148
A Variety of Things	149
Sleeping	150
Air Cleaners	151
Changing Times	152
Interior Decorating	153
Coffee	155
Snow and the Dentist	156
Chickens	157
Expectations	159

People

I Guess You Had to be There

The name for this collection is from a story I heard. I don't even remember the storyteller's name, but it was in the Owl's Nest Café in Hancock some time back. You'll notice I'm always a little vague on details.

Anyway, this guy was telling about Lyle when he was farming south of Hancock. Lyle was headed for town in his pickup, pulling a not-too-prosperous trailer loaded with grain. He had a flat by Bill Myers' place. Bill lived close to the road, and noticed that Lyle was having trouble getting his jack to work, so Bill took his jack and went out to help. He seemed to

understand the device, so Lyle let him raise the trailer while he went to get a lug wrench out of his pickup. It was the wrong size, so Bill went back to his shop and got the correct one.

As long as Bill had the wrench in his hand, Lyle let him remove the lug nuts and went for the spare in the pickup. Then he noticed that it, too, was flat, so Bill went back to his shop and got another wheel that would fit. Lyle loaded up the flat and his jack in his pickup while Bill tightened the wheel.

As Bill lowered his jack, Lyle climbed into his pickup, leaned out the door, and hollered at Bill, "It's all right this time. But next time, why don't you mind your own damn business."

One of the guys at the table went to get the coffeepot, another one picked up the sports page and started to read. Nobody seemed too interested in the story so the fellow kind of apologized by saying, "I guess you had to be there."

Memorial Day

The Sunday before Memorial Day Louise and I took an extended tour, at least for us it was extended. First we went North to Scandia Cemetery where some of my ancestors on my father's side are buried. This is where we plan to be installed, but hopefully not for a while. Then we went out to West Zion, where the biggest share of the rest of the relationship is planted. There are other places where I have ancestors, people I remember, but they are scattered around. Even in death they couldn't get together.

Those people actively engaged in agriculture probably don't have the time this spring, the season being like it is, but it is a time for remembering, a time to walk among the tombstones of families you know, and individuals you remember. And as time goes by it is not so much with sorrow as with a comfortable nostalgia for those times and those people. Sure we miss them, but they, like us, can and should be replaced.

Always looking for a bargain, we came home by way of Benson so we could stop at Hardee's and get a free cup of coffee. North of town we saw farmers working, some stuck deep in the mud. The equipment is getting larger now, and with all the sloughs that must be avoided, the detail work must be difficult. Those corn planters in the neighborhood of forty feet wide take more management than a team of horses and a two-row, even without the check wire.

Between the 17th of May, which is Norwegian Independence Day, and Memorial Day the crop in this area is supposed to be in the ground. That is according to some of my ancestors whose graves we visited today. It will be late this year, but we will survive. I'm sure of that.

Cliff Olson

I wrote this the day of Cliff's funeral. I admired him for many things, not the least of which was the way he used the last few years that his cancer grudgingly gave him.

My good friend Cliff will be buried today. We went to the visitation last night. The family and a lot of his friends were there, and the atmosphere was just what Cliff would have wanted. People were smiling and laughing, as will happen when there are a lot of good memories. I commented to one of the girls about seeing Cliff in a necktie, and she admitted it was unusual, but the clean fingernails bothered her more.

I remember Cliff telling me that he had just about decided to sell out the blacksmith shop when throw-away plow shares were invented and a lot of the farmers bought welders. But after he had made a list for the auctioneer, he thought there was just not enough stuff to make a decent looking sales bill. He said he would have been embarrassed to hang it up.

So he started selling a few short lines, putting in silo unloaders and cattle feeding tubes, spraying grain, erecting tin silos, and was busy enough so he forgot all about plow shares.

He had more than a passing interest in the board of trade also. I remember one time he told me he was looking down the highway, worrying that he might have to take delivery of a couple of truck loads of pork bellies.

He had the whole family involved in grain spraying. I recall he told me once he sent one of the boys out to spray a field for a farmer south of town, and when he came back, asked what he had sprayed, expecting it to be wheat, oats or maybe barley. When the boy told him flax, he asked if the farmer had the right chemical. He said no, he had just sprayed it the same as everything else. Cliff panicked, drove out to the farmer's place and saw the flax flat on the ground. He figured it was no use talking to the farmer, as he would hear plenty from him later. Nothing happened, and Cliff put it out of his mind. The next spring the guy stopped and asked Cliff to spray flax for him again. Then Cliff got up enough nerve to ask him how it had turned out last year. The farmer told him just fine, although it looked pretty tough right after you got done, "But," he said, "I figured you folks knew what you were doing."

I only remember one new piece of spraying equipment Cliff ever had. He and Les Johnson had a new highboy for a while, but Les tipped it over and broke his leg, and seemed to lose all his enthusiasm for the business after that. Les came into my yard one afternoon. Cliff was spraying with his Jeep, and they had a meeting down in my pasture for about an hour. Les left, Cliff finished the field and stopped at the house and told me they had just peacefully dissolved the partnership. An empty six-pack by the corner post marked the spot for a number of years.

I happened to be on hand when Cliff gave up on the old sprayer that his man Sylvan used to put on atrazine. He had pulled it for a number of years with an ancient M Farmall, and when that gave up, purchased a 460. Cliff and Sylvan were in the Lariat bar when Sylvan asked Cliff what he was figuring on doing with the tractor. He said he thought he could use it out at his place, and what did Cliff think it was worth. Sylvan had a little change lying on the bar in front of him, and Cliff reached over and swept it up into his hand. "That should be about right," he said, "You just bought a tractor."

Esterly

I've got a project started down in my basement that needs finishing, and I should get the upstairs hall painted. Now that I have gas for the string trimmer I should clear some of the grass away from the machine shed. But it's hard to get started.

At my age and physical condition, some things, some projects are more attractive than others, and sitting here at the keyboard is easy compared to painting or cutting grass.

This needs doing anyway. Linus and Esterly died the same week and I have some thoughts about their passing. I don't suppose what I write will have much meaning to those who didn't know Esterly, but here goes.

One was a little over ninety, the other a little less. Linus Pauling had two Nobel prizes, one for chemistry and another for peace. Esterly DeFrang had won no great awards and I suppose was not known outside this community. Esterly could play the piano or the violin by ear and was a carpenter for most of his life.

I do not know exactly what Linus discovered, and what effect that discovery may have had on me and mine. I do not know if we would be involved in even more war without his efforts.

I do know that Esterly helped me shingle and repair; he was always pleasant to be around, and people like him have built this country. Linus may have planned, but the Esterlys of this world are the ones who finally get things done.

When Esterly could no longer work at his trade, he still could help care for another, and did so. Life may not always have been easy for him; he was nearly deaf towards last, but managed, with the cooperation of Adeline, to make a go of it.

I'm getting of an age that I have to make some decisions about my life and I know that I can't be a Linus Pauling, but if I can be an Esterly, I'll be well satisfied.

Aging Gracefully

I was watching the Discovery Channel on television the other day and they had a thing on it about growing old, and the deterioration that comes with it. Now this is something I am familiar with, both from personal experience and from observing it in others. I could almost say I am an expert in that particular field.

There was an element of hope, though, because in the animal kingdom a few creatures seem to be immune. The tarantula, that big hairy spider, never seems to age, it just lives more or less the same until it dies of some illness or is killed. Some turtles are that way, too, they just go on and on, raising their families until they get a bad disease and die, or are squished on the road under a truck.

Even parts of the human body, they said, don't seem to age. The lining in one's intestines is replaced every two days, so that is always pretty much new. But then, if our brain was replaced like that, I suppose we would have to write ourselves a lot of notes, and would constantly be meeting new people. I would have a lot of trouble if memory only lasted two days. Mine makes it for about a week and that is bad enough. That is most weeks.

A friend visited with us a while back, and shared with me concerning his new toenails. I have a fungus under mine, that has caused them to grow thick, yellow and ugly, but as I most times wear shoes, no one complains. I assumed that it was just another one of those things that goes along with "maturity." The old medicines for this complaint had many undesirable side effects and worked very slowly. My friend had acquired a new pill, one that worked in only three months, did not upset his stomach or make his hair fall out, and he now has the toenails of a sixteen-year-old. They are thin, white, and easy to trim.

I envy him, and will try to get my insurance to pay for this miracle cure, as the pills are five bucks apiece and you need two a day. That is, if I remember.

Transportation

I recall a conversation while sitting in the Owl's Nest having coffee with Bennie and Otto Greiner and Chuck Myers. We started discussing how much easier it was to get around. Not like it used to be.

Bennie said the first car he remembers was a Mitchel that his father bought in 1920. It wasn't new; it had been made in 1916 and was really big, a seven-passenger with seats that folded down in different places and a huge eight-cylinder motor. It had a top and side curtains that slid on tracks so as to close out the weather to some extent.

Now nobody knew too much about cars, and the guy who sold it to them said that you should put in a quart of oil once in a while or something bad would happen. So whenever they went to town or to the neighbors, the driver would add a quart. Then one day it wouldn't start and they sent for the expert from Steinbring's Garage. He drained out 15 gallons of oil and showed them how to check the level. Then it ran just fine.

I mentioned this story about the Mitchel to Otto Shaefer and he said I should remove two cylinders and about ten gallons of the oil from my story, but I just write down what I hear, I don't edit. If you want accuracy, go someplace else.

Cars, of course, were mainly a summer time thing. Horses were more dependable. Otto mentioned Mortons having a runaway with the team that delivered cream to the creamery, and the horses ran only as far as the door where the cans were unloaded and stopped there. The horses couldn't break the habit.

Bennie said Levi Brown sent his hired man into Hancock one day to get a load of coal. Levi had a nice outfit, a fine team of sorrels and a good wagon. When his man didn't return on time Levi called town to see what was holding him up, and the guy at the coal shed said they hadn't seen him. They found the wagon later. The guy had traded it for a buggy in Benson, but it wasn't much use chasing after him, as they didn't have anything that could go any faster then that team of sorrels.

Livestock went to market on foot if you lived close enough to the shipping association pens by the railroad tracks and had enough kids to herd them. Otherwise you loaded them up in a wagon and hauled them to town.

The discussion centered on the honesty of the various agents for the shipping associations. Generally someone from the family would ride down to the stock yards in St. Paul in the caboose to see how the cattle sold, and try to see that the commission men were reasonably honest. Chuck mentioned getting a ride in a locomotive one time to get a little closer to the pens where his family's cattle were, and how unusual it was for anyone connected with the railroad to show any concern at all for a farmer. He was young at the time, and the engineer must have had a kind heart.

Barbra

I was listening to an interview on the radio where the interviewee, if that's what you call him, was a big shot from Las Vegas. He was one of the bosses of the new MGM Grand, whatever that is. They plan on having, he said, about fifty big events throughout the year, and the one he was talking about was a Christmas concert he had scheduled with Barbra Streisand.

I listened a little closer then, as I like Barbra, even though she spells her name funny. Then the guy said that when the event was advertised, they got one million calls asking for reservations in the first twenty-four hours. A million--that's a one and six zeros. All the tickets were gone after the first six hours, and they would have been sold out much sooner if they had had another five hundred telephone operators taking orders. Barbra's fine, but are people nuts? Can't they stay home with their families at Christmas?

I don't know how many people that place will hold, but imagine it will be quite a few. I suppose the tickets will cost an arm and a leg, as this is one of the characteristics of a Barbra concert. As you may have guessed, I am not going. I did not go to WeeFest either, but attended the horticulture event at West Central, and plan on going to the Stevens County fair, and the Herman Iron Pour. So you see, I get around, at least to some extent.

Funerals

When one is a pallbearer two days in a row you begin to consider your own mortality, and realize that this life is not a permanent thing. My cousin Lillian was 85, about 17 years older than me, so that gives me a little time, but the next day we buried Bob Swanson, who was 65, a few years younger than I.

You realize that this is your generation when people want to know something about that person in the casket and they ask you. You are finally the remains of that generation and it is disquieting, to say the least.

Things I remembered at those two funerals, the things that came to mind sitting there are not important, but when I am gone, I wonder if anyone else will know or care about those events. I remember being at a Church camp at Green Lake near Spicer when I was in high school. Lillian was the camp nurse. Her husband, Pastor Arnold Olson, was there in some capacity, and I was supposed to be sort of a proctor of one of the cabins.

I was not up to the challenge of keeping discipline in this group of boys not much younger than I so a pastor was moved into our cabin to keep good order. He was less than successful, and was forced to spend most of the night getting the youngsters out of the lake and back into bed. Lillian came into the cabin while he was out enforcing good order, short sheeted his bed and filled it liberally with sand and clamshells.

The pastor woke me with his loud exclamations when he came in at about three in the morning, dropped his pants and placed his bare, weary bottom onto the mess in his bed.

With Bobby, I remember having rock fights in the street by the school in Hancock. Richard Cushing, Bob's two sisters and I would divide up. Some would go upstairs in Cushing's barn, the rest would be out in the gravel road, and we would throw rocks at each other. We were not angry with each other; we didn't even consider the possibility that we could get hurt. We just did it. This was before television; we entertained ourselves.

These are not important things, I suppose, so if no one remembers them, it is of no consequence. And I suppose it does not speak too well of me that these are the types of things I think of at these somber times. But then, I think that there are more things like this in our lives. They make up a greater part of our lives than the important stuff.

I suppose I should have been thinking about Lillian nursing in some hospital, or playing the organ in church, and Bobby hunting, or spearing fish in the winter, or working with a carpenter or at the concrete plant, but I can't help the way my mind works. And I wonder what people will think about at my funeral.

At Lillian's funeral Carolyn Pederson sang `Den Store Hvide Flok', and `I Have a Friend' beautifully. Both songs were in Norwegian, of which I understand little, but as always, they affected me.

But the last song's melody reminded me of something we sang years ago, in happy times.

> Bill Grogan's goat was feeling fine,
> ate three red shirts right off the line.
> Bill took a stick, gave him a whack,
> and tied him to the railroad track.
> The whistle blew, the train drew nigh,
> that poor old goat was soon to die,
> He gave a cough of awful pain,
> coughed up those shirts,
> and flagged the train.

Lillian would have enjoyed it.

Wee Wee

When I woke up this morning, and it was raining, I turned on the bedside radio to a FM station to eliminate the static. I got in on about the middle of an interview with a lady

13

who lived in a small city in southern Sweden. She had environmental concerns about a little lake by the town.

Nitrates seemed to be the problem in the lake, and she felt that the town sewage treatment system had no trouble handling everything that was put into it except the urine. For the sake of delicacy, I will use the description that we used when I was young and it was necessary to distinguish between these bodily functions, number one and number two.

I understood that they tested the output of the system many times a day, and noticed a leap in the nitrate levels right away in the morning. She figured this was when everyone in town was using their facilities. The lady had come to the conclusion that this consisted mainly of number one, and that the main load of number two would come later in the day.

I have never been there. I don't know how they do things in Sweden, or how well they regulate all these functions. Here in Hodges Township, I would hate to try to predict what anyone was doing at any particular time of the day.

The lady's solution, then, was to have what she called a "Wee Wee Holiday." For one day everyone would go in the woods or in the garden, and if they were too bashful, they should use a pot and carry it out into the woods to empty it. Then, if nitrate levels fell, she would have proved her theory that more work had to be done on how the system should deal with number one.

She was Swedish of course, and Swedes do have a tendency to worry about things most others don't and find unusual solutions to problems.

Migrating Like the Falcons

Got a phone call from some friends last night. We had been wondering about them, as they travel around quite a bit and generally stop here and report every so often. They ski, they polka, they pick berries and make stuff, while Louise and I are sedentary, have no spirit of adventure, and can always be counted on to be here, or within five or so miles of here.

Like I say, these folks travel around a lot, and are getting a little long in the tooth, like all of us of that generation. And as with most who attain great age, they have more physical problems. A couple of years ago it was his turn to have surgery, and now it is evidently her turn.

They called from Rochester. Like anyone with any sense, they seek medical treatment in Minnesota where we have real doctors and hospitals.

Anyway, it was her turn to have difficulty keeping up with the hectic pace of retirement, and she mentioned to me something she had seen in Rochester that appealed to her. On one of the taller buildings a place had been fixed for a pair of peregrine falcons to nest. A television monitor had been installed so people in the lobby could amuse themselves watching the birds killing and eating pigeons, feeding their young and so forth.

Carol learned a fact about these birds, a thing that sounded very good to her at this point in time. She learned that while they mate for life, and share the responsibility of raising their young, they migrate separately. So when the kids are ready to go on their own, the old folks say to each other, "So long, see you in the spring" and go their separate ways, and at their own pace.

Superman

I have always liked Superman. His latest reincarnation on television, in Lois and Lane, is a little nicer. He seems to fly more realistically than when he was first on the tube. But he is still highly moral, always on the side of right, and always wins. We need somebody like that.

Of course he has that problem with krypton, but generally somebody will help him out so he gets his strength back in time to save the day.

I suppose the reason I admire Superman so much is that I have a desire to be like him. Not that I would care much for being able to leap tall buildings in a single bound, but that x-ray vision would really come in handy when playing cards. The only similarity I have with him now is that I have my own version of krypton-- penicillin and that nasal decongestant in a squirt bottle, pseudoephedrine hydrochloride. Either one can render me helpless.

I suppose my love for Superman would indicate I have been watching too much TV, and my brain is beginning to rot. This is a possibility. I am elderly and susceptible to that sort of thing, but Superman isn't responsible. Compared to some of the other stuff I see, like the O.J. trial and the killing in Africa and Bosnia, a flying man in a cape and tights makes a lot of sense.

You see, we have to make up our own heroes these days. When we find somebody in real life that we admire, they generally disappoint us. Either by something they do, or fail to do, or are submerged in accusations until we don't know what to believe. Now they are even going back to dig up stuff on some of our old time heroes. So you see, we need Superman.

Fertilizer

I have a little blue folder that came in the mail the other day, offering a course in manure management. This is new to me. I have hauled manure, pitched manure, spread manure. I even spent a good part of my life wading in manure, but not to my knowledge have I ever managed manure. It would be more accurate to say that manure managed me.

I consider myself more or less an expert in this field. I am familiar with most types of the product, from the hard packed variety, caused by either cold weather or the type of bedding used, and the type of livestock, through the various consistencies, varying from so thick that you can almost, but not quite walk on, down to a brown liquid that gets waves on it in windy weather. They each require their special technique in handling.

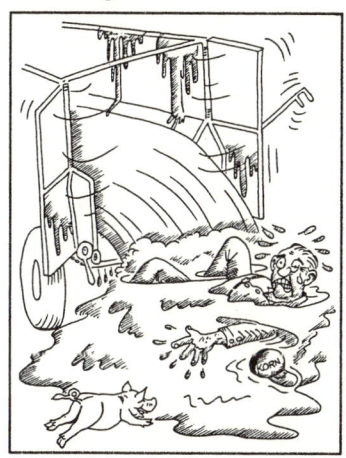

The tiniest mistake can be unpleasant, especially with the juicy kind. I remember one time I helped a friend of mine, Harold Anderson, remove a little of that kind of stuff from his cattle lot early one spring. My loader had a bucket on it that rolled back quite a ways so it would hold about two or three barrels of the wet stuff. His plan was to load it into a silage box, as that was tighter than the manure spreader, and put it on his garden. We got his Dokken box brim full, he pulled it to the place and removed the little narrow door on the bottom of the big swinging doors on the back to let the stuff run out. It was just a shade too thick, only a dribble ran out, so he decided to open the big doors.

Now, if you are familiar with these boxes, they had two latches and two bars that locked down into slots, holding the doors together and shut. He unlocked the top latch, and then kicked the bottom one open. His feet slipped out from under him, he fell flat on his back, the doors banged open, and the entire load, well..... you can imagine what happened.

We were close to the house, so he undressed outside in spite of the rather brisk weather, and we quit for the day. He never found his cap.

Rabbits

This story isn't really about rabbits; it's more about rocks. I believe it, because it was told to me by a guy I don't think would lie to me, not intentionally anyway, and it seems likely, as I know the people involved and the place where it is supposed to have happened. I suppose I could check it out some more, but that requires more effort than I am willing to expend, like the politicians say, at this point in time.

Fred had a lot of rocks on that quarter north of where I live. He had even bought an old Allis Chalmers crawler tractor with a dozer on it to dig holes and bury rocks. For years he waged war on those rocks, spring and fall, digging, picking and burying them. This was supposed to have happened one day when he and his son were out on this never-ending project.

Anyway, what happened was they had filled a trailer with rocks and Paul went to empty it. Fred was resting, sitting on a big stone, elbows resting on his knees, half asleep, letting the breeze blow through the front of his overalls, as they kind of bagged out when he leaned forward. The dog, like all farm dogs, had followed the tractor, and as they came back into the

field, scared up a rabbit. It must have been a slow rabbit and a fast dog, because the rabbit decided that it needed a place to hide, and the only thing it could see that wasn't moving, that offered hiding place, was Fred. According to what was told to me, the rabbit jumped right into Fred's pants, scaring him half to death.

I might check this out later, but even if it isn't true, you've got to admit it's possible.

Belly Buttons

When no one you know real well is watching, do you act differently? We know we can get away with things in front of strangers that our friends would never let us do. For instance, wearing clothes while on vacation that we would never wear around home. Not me, of course, I am always the same. Or maybe that is because I never go any place where I am among strangers.

For example, I have a friend who bought a toupee. A nice rug, quite expensive and natural looking. He cannot wear it around people he knows, as they are used to him not having hair, and will treat him unmercifully bad. He knows this and has used it only for trips to faraway places. People are a lot like animals, if they see something a little different, they pick, pick, pick. Eva, a German exchange student who currently is staying with our daughter in Wisconsin, brought this to my attention. She is far enough from home so that she feels she can do things that would not be acceptable back home. She is agitating for an opportunity to bungee jump, and going to Eau Claire to have her navel pierced. She says that it is cheaper here than in Germany. It's nice to know we are ahead of the Europeans in this art. Our daughter is going along with the navel piercing as that does not seem as life threatening and may distract the girl from the more dangerous pursuits. Of course, even among strangers I would not feel the need to do either one of these things. They seem pointless, painful and dangerous, but then I am old, and have no spirit of adventure.

Shakespeare

I was force fed a little Shakespeare in school, many years ago, and didn't particularly enjoy it. I got to thinking about that a while back and started to wonder how come. I figure I'm just as cultured as the next guy. How come it made so little sense to me?

When you have a problem, when you need answers, go to the library. I checked out a book, *The Complete Works of William Shakespeare*, and started to investigate.

The answer was pretty obvious. Even today, Englishmen talk funny, and back in the fifteen hundreds, when old Will was writing, it was even worse. If a farmer from Minnesota is going to get anything out of his plays, they will have to be translated into Minnesotan and the scenes and nationalities changed so we can identify with his characters and their problems.

Take Romeo and Juliet, for instance. I guess they were from Italy, and probably a little too emotional for a Norwegian to understand. It starts out, these two families, the Capulets and the Montagues, are fighting with swords and killing each other a lot for no particular reason until it upsets Prince Escalus, who is kind of like the county commissioner. He tells them that if they keep on making a commotion he is going to do something drastic. This is not a man you want to fool around with.

Norwegians can't relate to this. They never fight unless they are drunk and then not very well. We may give each other hard looks, but that is about all.

It's a shame when a good story goes to waste because it's so hard to understand. It needs interpretation and maybe a few little modifications. Kind of bring it up to date.

The language has to be fixed. What kind of a Minnesotan would say something like, "I would thou wert so happy by thy stay, To hear true shift. Come madam, let's away." I hope I didn't quote something dirty.

Maybe we could move it from Verona to some more local place, like maybe Swift Falls or Sunburg. That's far enough away so it's a little exotic, but still understandable. Then maybe it could be a Swedish family and a Norwegian family that didn't get along. Well, you get the idea. Of course, I don't see either one of the lovers killing themselves, or hollering and waving their arms like I see Shakespearean actors do on television. Just make it into a nice, gentle Ole and Lena story.

Country School

I would prefer to do my research by listening to people. Then I can excuse my errors by saying that they must have been wrong, or I must have misunderstood.

The other day in Senior Citizens Center, Otto Schaefer recited a poem that he said the children in school district 65 used in 1923 as part of a Christmas program. He said he remembers helping ten Schaefers and fifteen Greiners, (more than one family) sing this song as they wrapped tissue paper streamers around a "North Pole" that had been erected in the schoolhouse. About forty students, a few Stettners and some Millers, were also included.

I decided that for once I would check the information and went to the Stevens County Museum to see if they had any records of #65. No luck. But Tami Plank took me to the basement and brought out a box that contained records from #45, which was located very close to #65, and #53, another near neighbor. Fascinating. I now know stuff about a lot of you people out there that I'll bet you wouldn't want me to repeat.

On the plus side, I found that Max Huntley did well in his examinations, passing out of the eighth grade easily in 1912. He got an 87, only needed a 65, so he was the top in his class. Then, in 1933, his daughter Lois was promoted from second to third grade by virtue of her straight A average. Gert Eckstein made it from third to fourth the same way, all A's.

I didn't find out much about Gert's athletic ability, but Lois brought fame to District 45 in 1937 by taking third place in the broad jump at the county school field day.

The teacher made little notes in the record about the kids. Some were charitable, "Could work harder." Others were less so. "Hard to manage and lazy," or "Very mischievous" or a somewhat cryptic "Needs watching". Thing is, I know some of these people, and they turned out rather well. I guess it was a good thing that somebody kept on watching. Slip me a few bucks and I'll give you names, if I can remember them.

In that period, changes in record keeping and quality of equipment showed up. The teacher's want list in 1912 was simple, a new dustpan, a wash basin and stand, some towels. By 1933 they needed a soccer ball, a kittenball, and a "bubbler" to drink from. No more bucket and common dipper.

By 1938, #53 had 100 square feet of blackboard, a Lennox furnace, a six-volume encyclopedia, three dictionaries and kerosene stove for hot lunches. Real class.

I intend to go back into that basement, and find out more about you people, and maybe your ancestors. District Nine, my Alma Mater, has few records, and I have them hidden away.

If you ask I am sure that Otto will recite that poem for you.

Staying in One Place

Great grandpa was the adventurer in the family. He loaded up wife and children and left Norway about 1850 to come to America. Then his son, my grandfather had enough adventure left in his soul to come here from Kenyon, Minnesota to homestead in the early 1870s. Since then his descendants seem to be pretty much satisfied to stay where they are.

We live in the house where I was born. My father and most of my uncles and aunts on his side of the family were born here too, not in this house, but in one that stood just about where this one stands. Our children are here only occasionally, but I think enough so you could say four generations have inhabited the place. In this neighborhood I think that is kind of a record. Well over a hundred years of Rasmussons. Not that they accomplished much, but then they didn't get in many people's way either. One has to take pride in what is available, and for us, that is pretty much it.

Then I heard on the radio about a place called Cheddar, in England. In 1903 they found a skeleton in a cave near this town, and put it in the local museum. The people are proud of their cave person, and wanted to keep the bones safe. Some professors at the University of Bristol tested it later, after the carbon dating process was invented, and found it was about 7000 years old.

Now they have this test for DNA, so they took a sample of the old bones, and then samples from some families that live in the area, and found one guy, a fellow named Adrian Target, who the tests indicate is related to the cave person on his mother's side. Ain't science wonderful? This would give the guy a family tree considerably longer than the English royal family, who can only go back about 1200 years. If they fooled around then like they do now, I wonder how accurate that can be.

Seven thousand years, and still hanging around the same place. And people give me crap about not wanting to go south for the winter. I've only been here about seventy years.

Ross

This Thanksgiving it will be almost 60 years since my uncle Ross died. My mother and dad had gone someplace else that day, but Ross and I had been with his sister Ida and her husband Fred Heuer who lived on Starvation Hill, a farm on the south side of Lake Minnewaska. I liked to go there because in the summer I could use the wagon Fred used to take milking utensils down the hill to the barn and coast from the house nearly to the water. If there was snow, it was even better, as the rocks and stumps were covered and less maneuvering was necessary with his big sled.

Fred and Ida had no children, as they had been married late in life. My grandfather Lars said Ida got so old she had to marry a German. Fred fished more than he farmed, and Ida smoked fish, canned fish, pickled fish, and when she had company, they ate fish. This was not a prosperous time, back in the thirties, but some way or other we were happy and well fed.

Ross and I were together a lot, we shared a room upstairs in this house. He was a bachelor, my dad's partner in the farm, and it was a terrible shock to my 11-year-old mind when he died of a heart attack that afternoon on the floor of our kitchen. For years afterwards I would think I saw him across the street in town, or in a car we met on the road.

Ross, or Rasmus as it said on his birth certificate, was thirty when he and his brother Christ, five years his junior, homesteaded near Ambrose in Northwestern North Dakota. My Dad was only sixteen at the time, but he and Lars farmed until the adventurers sold out and came home. Christ found a wife out in that country, but Ross was less fortunate.

Christ played the violin, kind of, and Ross was much desired to sing at weddings and funerals. Norwegian songs, mostly, without accompaniment. Like I say, he was popular, but it embarrassed me to hear him, and I would prefer to be some place else when he sang. But then I'm no musician.

Ross always had a pretty good car, as being a bachelor gave him more time and more undesignated cash. Every year he would take a bath, brush his teeth, and go to Minneapolis. A couple of his buddies would go along, and they would be gone for about three or four days. These were generally called business trips. Shipping association or school board things had to be attended to, but they generally found time to go to a burlesque theater. I know this from some of the things that came back with Ross from these trips.

One time in particular, I found a large snapshot of Ross and his two friends sitting around a little table, each with a glass of something in their hand, and a very lightly dressed young lady, wearing just a few feathers and a couple of tassels, in each of their laps. Ross looked cool, but the other two, the married ones, had very guilty expressions on their faces. In my youth and inexperience, I showed the picture to my mother, and she destroyed it. She explained that she had just saved the lives of these two gentlemen, and they would never be aware of it.

Conception

It must be some over 40 years ago, out of respect I will not say how many over, my friends, newly married, stayed one night at this house on the way to more schooling in either Wisconsin or Missouri, I forget which. This was before Louise and I were married, so I was living with my parents here. Some time later, I got a card from them announcing the birth of their daughter. My mother, who was of the generation that kept track of this kind of thing, thought a while, and announced that it was exactly nine months since they had stayed with us. I did not dispute this, as she had a knack for knowing what was happening to people she knew. At least I could never get away with anything, and I am sure that magic of hers extended to anyone who spent time under our roof.

We have discussed this prescience of my mother with this couple at various times over the years. They say that while they can't say for sure, it's a distinct possibility that she may have been correct, and they wonder about some of the various ramifications of this, if it can be proven.

If the issue of this union becomes famous, the birthplace will have a monument erected, so why not, if documented, the place of conception? If an exceptionally fine, successful person is born, will a flood of other newlyweds rush to use the facilities? If the child had been less than satisfactory, could a claim be made against the homeowner's liability policy? On astrological charts, the place and time of birth are very significant, but by that time most of the factors that make up the character of the child is well established. You would think that the place of conception would be much more important, if you take that stuff seriously. You can see, a lot of questions come up.

Consideration

People have to pay attention and show consideration for others. I was coming into Morris from Hancock the other day, a nice warm day, by the way. I stopped for a red light by the Standard station, and a pickup rolled by on my right side and made a right turn. It may have stopped before turning, I didn't notice, as I was watching a mature gentleman on a bicycle go by in front of me. He saw the pickup at the last minute and turned left. Fortunately no one was coming in the other lane. He nearly fell from the bike, and the pickup proceeded on; I don't think they were even aware of the incident.

Happily, it turned out all right, no damage, unless maybe a little spotting in the gentleman's undies, but no one was hurt, no property damaged, but it could have been bad, even at low speeds. We've got to pay more attention.

Now, having attained great age without running over anyone with my automobile, and not being run over myself, I am going to endeavor to pay more attention. Try to keep up with the traffic, not get too angry with that SOB hanging on my rear bumper, and stay alert.

We are fortunate here. Traffic is generally light, and this lowers the need for constant vigilance, but we should not be lulled into thinking that we don't have to pay any attention, that everyone else can take care of themselves.

I hear of people on the freeways of California shooting at people out of frustration, and I can understand that. That is why I make it a practice not to carry a gun in my car.

I remember an incident on Interstate 94 coming west toward Hudson, Wisconsin. It had snowed, a lot of wet, slushy snow, and the cars were driving only about 30 miles an hour, following single file in the two tracks a truck had made in the right lane. Suddenly a pickup with huge tires came roaring by us in the deep snow in the left lane, spraying all our windshields with slush, and disappearing over the hill ahead.

A few miles further down the road we saw the pickup buried in snow up to the door handles in the ditch in the central median. I saw the first car that passed it open a window and give a one-finger salute, the next car the same, and so forth down the line.

A small thing, but I'm sure it made us all feel a little better.

Weather

Busy, Busy, Busy

I have been instructed by the vet to feed the dog a heart worm pill once a month, and at the same time apply a squirt or two of a chemical that will kill the lice and wood ticks she is inclined to accumulate. In order to remember to do this, I decided to do it on the day I read the electric meter and send in the check. I realize this is quite a bit for an old fellow to do all in one day, but I figured that if I start early I could get it done. Maybe have to skip a card game, but I can catch up on that later.

This has been pretty much the pattern each summer, and it has worked pretty well, until today. We had an emergency. Louise complained of a bad smell in the kitchen and turned the problem over to me. Evidently, some time in the recent past, a mouse had passed away in our pantry. I hope it died of loneliness, but I doubt it.

After repairing the light in the pantry, which had not functioned for some time, I found the animal back in the corner under some stuff. We had to remove a couple of generations of pots and pans from the place and then on hands and knees scrub the shelves and floor with some stuff that smelled almost as bad as the mouse. My trap line has not been productive for quite a while, and that is encouraging, but now I suppose I will have to give it more attention.

As the days get shorter and the temperature cools here in the country, mice like to move into the house. We make it as difficult for them as we can, but they seem to find a way.

Some of the mice have white chests and feet and are no problem. They will go out of their way to get caught in a trap or clubbed to death with a broom, but the little, brown sneaky mice are a different deal altogether. They seem to need people to survive. I have suggested a cat, but Louise says that I am her mouser, and she will not get a house cat until I can no longer handle the job.

Dry Winter Air

Louise's sister Jean showed us a questionnaire this morning, I think it was from St. Olaf college, and one of the questions was about how one felt about being Norwegian. The questionnaire wanted to know if we were ashamed of it, or if we were proud of it, and if we were aware of the fact that Norwegians were better than every other nationality. Silly question, everybody knows that. I guess somebody else is snowbound and under occupied, that they would have to ask questions about things that are common knowledge everywhere.

I, in my great Norse wisdom, have decided that it is no use to complain about the snow. I haven't gone so far as to pretend that I enjoy it yet, but have decided just to ignore it. While the snow has me imprisoned in our house, there are a few things that I can't ignore.

When the weather is this cold for this long, the air in our house gets as dry as a desert. Downstairs it isn't so bad. We have a big humidifier that pumps about three gallons of water into the air every day, which seems to be enough to keep the wooden furniture from falling apart, but the moisture doesn't seem to get upstairs where we sleep. So when I wake up in the morning, my mouth and nose are dry as dust.

When we are snowbound, I have nothing else to do, so end up spending a lot of time in bed. I wake up, and my mouth and nose are not merely full of cotton, like one would expect but with saliva in my mouth congealed until it is like cement. I am afraid I am going to dry up all the way, and will catch on fire.

This morning as I swung my feet out of bed, one foot

caught on the window curtain, and it took me some time to get it disconnected. I noticed that the calluses on the soles of my feet have gotten so dry that they stick to the carpet like Velcro. I will have to grease them, or I will never be able to get my socks on and off.

It's Cold!

I suppose I shouldn't complain, I don't have to carry baskets of silage out to the feed bunks for the cattle, after chopping the frozen stuff loose from the walls in the silo and pitching it down the chute. The water comes when I turn on the faucet, I have neither to pump it nor carry it. Still, twenty-five below zero is not pleasant. The hairs in my nose get brittle, and it makes me sneeze. The weatherman says it's going to get worse.

Chuck told me that he had waded through the snow to check the fuel in the barrel behind his house, breaking through the crust with every step, and he had been concerned on how he was going to get back to the house, as he got so out of breath. He said he hoped the folks would have the good sense, if he died back there, to leave him lay until he got stiff, as he would be easier to pick up when he didn't bend in the middle. Chuck is always considerate of others.

Louise and I went into town this morning, just to prove to ourselves that we could make it, that we were able to conquer the weather, the snow, and the environment in general. The Owl's Nest was pretty full, others had the same idea. We are all shaped the same, round and tightly packed, wearing all the clothes we own. Faces and the degree of tallness or shortness are all that distinguish one from another. The layered, unisex look is in here in Hancock.

The Blizzard of 1996

It is Thursday, the 18th of January, and the weather is not nice at all. It is 2:30 in the afternoon and I have yet to put on my pants. I am thankful that I am an old person with no responsibilities, so I can just doze in my recliner and watch stupid things on television. For instance, I just learned that Lisa Marie Presley-Jackson has filed for divorce from Michael. And Fergie, the duchess of York owes about a million bucks and the Queen is not going to bail her out any more. But I do not have to worry about that, and I don't have to worry about where I should be or what I should be doing.

I have always prided myself in being able to keep from being bored, but now am starting to wonder. Outside of scooping up a pile of snow that had blown in through a crack in a patio door and feeding the dog, I have done nothing. I must remind myself that I am old, and do not need to do anything. I can be almost like a congressman or a senator, and just live on the efforts of others. Someone else will keep the electricity coming and others will plow the roads when the wind stops. I have most of the politicians' advantages, except for free health care and huge salaries and unlimited free travel at our expense. I have another advantage, a blessing for others as well as myself, I do not have to give speeches.

The radio says that the wind chill in Fargo is eighty below and the interstate highway is closed. I can see why. But then we see television weather people standing outside in the cold, struggling to stand in the furious, biting wind, telling us how bad it is. The wind blowing across their microphones makes them hard to understand. Is this their idea or are they forced to do it by some cruel supervisor? Why do they do this? Haven't they windows they can look out of? Why is it necessary to add drama to a blizzard, one of nature's most dramatic features?

November 11th, 1940 my folks, Henry Fenner and I spent a good part of the day outside trying to move a sheep buck from the barn to a little shed a couple of hundred feet away. Late in the afternoon my father discovered he was out of chewing tobacco, and walked along a fence a mile to the neighbors to get a supply. We did chores, chopped wood, listened on the party line telephone, and went to bed when it got dark.

The weather looks just the same, but a lot of other things are different.

Snow Plowing

I think I've figured out why some of us like to live here in the frozen north. We are reluctant to admit it, but we really like snow and cold weather. We pretend we don't and we complain about it, but actually, we can't get along without it. It gives us a time out once in a while. It changes our schedules, and we secretly like to have Mother Nature give us an excuse once in a while not to go someplace that we would really rather not go, or do something that we don't want to do, but can't think of an excuse.

Even when it's twenty below and the wind is howling we secretly enjoy it, especially if the storm doesn't last too long.

I've noticed that after a big snow storm, everybody who lives in the country thinks up an excuse to see if they can get to town. If they live in the country, and if they have a four wheel drive, they will be out trying it before the snowplows are out. Kind of a victory over the elements, I suppose.

Royce the farmer put his snowplow on the front of my old four-wheel drive and I think it's fun to plow through the snow and see it flying out of the way, into the ditch. The blade can be set straight, and I can push snow into big piles, which is not really a good idea, as then it takes longer for it to melt, but it is fun anyway. I used to get a lot of satisfaction blowing snow with a tractor, even if I knew it wasn't going to do much good, the wind would fill the yard up again right away. It made you feel as if you were doing something constructive.

Now, you understand when I was feeding cattle, it was twenty below for two weeks at a time and the snow and the wind never stopped, I didn't enjoy it, I am not completely nuts, but blizzards, spaced out properly, and lasting not too overly long, are really nice.

This morning I drove into Morris, and I saw something that proved my theory. My neighbor Donny has a new snow blower, one you walk behind, and he keeps his driveway immaculate with it. But this morning he was on top of a big drift by his garage shoveling snow down on the driveway so he could blow it back up. I'm going to have to talk to him about that, I know it's fun, but there are limits.

Big Day

I really got into action today. After being gone a little while, getting home and getting enough grass mowed so the neighbors can find our house, I went to get a haircut. Harold the barber is getting better, but still not quite healthy enough to operate his clippers, leaving only one barber in the county, so I went to a beauty shop. Is that the right word for one of those places? This is a new experience for me. The place looks and smells differently than what I am used to, but Lila assured me that many men go there, and I shouldn't be afraid. She explained that the ladies in there are used to men getting haircuts and will hardly notice my presence.

Such, however was not the case. When I came in, the hair on the two ladies in the chairs stood right up on end. Jan and Lila tried to explain that it was just because it was in the process of being repaired, but I wonder.

Anyway, I got a haircut, no foo foo water like Harold uses, but that is OK, I can get along without that stuff. I got trimmed in time to bum a free meal at the corn growers plot, and as we had a free supper last night courtesy of the bank, now all I have to worry about is where do I eat free tomorrow.

I listened to the various seed corn reps describe the varieties in the plots, and was amazed to hear that every one was either a first or second in the county yield trials. They had 16 kinds of corn there, and they all looked good, so I suppose that is why nobody wanted to claim third, fourth, and so on.

When I was young, anyone who claimed forty bushels an acre around here was most likely stretching the truth. I only wish that we had made as much progress in human ethics as we have in corn genetics.

Yvonne Simon from the Minnesota corn growers was there with a lawn mower and a pickup that burned 85% ethanol. We all smelled of the exhaust and were impressed. She explained the progress being made in the promotion of ethanol in gasoline, and a little about how some of the oil companies are using half truths to discourage its use.

So, you can see I had a busy day.

Wasting Time

Sometime soon the people at NASA are going to get their rocket fixed and are going up to get that American lady that has been living with the Russians in their space station for the last six months. She did not expect to stay there that long, but technical difficulties have delayed her return. The news report mentioned that they were going to bring some needed supplies along as they were running low on grub. I wonder about sanitary conditions there. I would hate to go six months without a bath. I know Louise would hate it.

Now, some people might wonder what a person would do, how they would spend their time, locked up in a space capsule for six months, with the same people to talk to, and nothing much to do. I could handle that job, I've had the training and experience. For me it would be a piece of cake.

I have never been one to make very efficient use of my time. I have a tendency to waste both time and effort doing things that do not need doing, and then, sometimes, just doing nothing at all, when I should be busy. The clock just seems to run faster for me than it does for anyone else.

Some time ago, Louise and I came up behind a neighbor and his wife at a railroad crossing. It was a long coal train, moving slowly, so I shut off the motor and kind of slumped down in the seat, resting my eyes. In the car in front of us, the wife pulled a file folder from the seat, passed a few papers to her husband behind the wheel, and it looked to me like they were doing a little work on their income tax. The end of the train passed, and away they went, having accomplished way more than we did.

At the auction the other day, I was standing staring off into space, wasting time as usual, and I noticed a young lady open a large purse and take out several pieces of cloth and a scissors and begin cutting out little parts for something she intended to make. When the auctioneer got over to what she was interested in, she packed up her stuff, and moved over to bid. Not a wasted motion, I admire people like that. They make me a little nervous, but I admire them.

I have excuses now, at this point in my life, for moving slowly and accomplishing little. I will not bore you with tales about all my physical limitations. Most of the people I associate with can top me in this regard, but they don't set any speed records either. I am of a generation that has accomplished about what it is going to accomplish, so I think we may as well just sit back and relax.

What I Hear When I Shut Up

I had an interesting couple of days at the senior citizen center in Hancock. I'm finding that it pays to shut up and listen once in a while.

Gene Eckstein told us about the circumstances that caused him to join the navy back in 1936. He had been working on a farm for twelve dollars a month, from way too early to way too late, and the twenty-one bucks that the navy promised looked pretty good. He learned to be a diver, putting on the rubber suit and big iron hat and going under water to scrape barnacles off the water intakes on the ship, and got another twenty bucks a month for that. Lots better than milking cows.

He served on the Langley, a converted collier that had been made into the first American aircraft carrier. Later it had half the flight deck removed and it was used to haul aircraft and served as a refueling station for PBY's, the old flying boats. It was sunk by the Japanese early in the war in the south Pacific.

Gene said the ship was not exactly state of the art, and was not balanced right. In a storm off Cape Hatteras, it got to rolling so badly the whole crew had to stay up on the flight deck, running back and forth to the high side of the ship, to prevent it from turning over.

Joe Wiese said that the biggest thing he ever got to ride in was his Uncle Leo's Pierce Arrow. It was a huge thing, the radiator cap about ten feet from the windshield. Joe was only about fifteen, and it really made him feel like a big shot. The car had come from Chicago with a load of merchandise, and Leo either owned it or had the use of it for a while.

This was prior to 1933, and Leo was both a retailer and a wholesaler of spirits. Joe said booze came in gallon cans, three to a box, and Leo paid a buck a gallon. He retailed it for fifty cents a half-pint. I don't know who furnished the bottles. Anyway, a really good mark up. Chuck Myers said he had found a cache of empty gallon cans by the underpass, and tried to sell them to the druggist, but he wouldn't buy them because they were just a little small, held only about three quarts. Couldn't even trust your bootlegger in those days.

Now I try and get these things down correctly, but I am not 100 percent in the memory department, so any questions will have to be referred to Gene, Joe and Chuck.

Pocket Gophers

I worry about the pocket gophers in the Red River Valley. Our discussion group went over their problem in the cafe the other day, and we wonder how many survived the flood. Pocket gophers do not climb trees, at least I have never seen one doing it, and while they live rather dull, uninteresting lives, they are still one of God's creatures, and are our responsibility.

Should we have made more of an effort to save them? Should we have an inventory up in the valley, sort of a gopher census, to decide if we need to restock the area?

We have plenty of them here, and I am sure a lot of them will be willing, with a little encouragement, to relocate. I have heard of no government programs addressing this problem. The Red Cross and the Salvation Army seem uninterested, so if anything is to be done, I guess it is up to us as individuals to capture and transport a few gophers to the Red River Valley.

Hauling them could get to be a problem, as I hear from people who claim to know that they are not social animals. They prefer solitude and only on rare occasions seek one another's company. This means that they will have to be transported one at a time if they are to arrive in a contented state. Not a happy state, I guess they are never happy. They are industrious but morose beasts and it is not in their nature to be happy.

One of the gentlemen in our group was of the opinion that gophers build little domed residences down under the ground, substantial enough to trap a bubble of air, and there they can remain for a long period of time under water and emerge none the worse for the experience. They would use the time for reflection and contemplation and would not be bored or get excited and attempt to swim for it. Others doubted this, and I guess we will have to wait for the results of the inventory to know for sure how many survived

The Weather

This has been a terrible winter. No spectacular cold, not a terrible lot of snow, no long lasting blizzards or ice storms, but enough of all the bad stuff, so that when you put it together, it was just a plain rotten winter. So I was relieved when it warmed up to 70 on my thermometer yesterday. Then a little rain shower last night and the weather people are talking about snow again. It's not supposed to be like that when it is income tax time. How much is a person supposed to endure?

It wouldn't bother me so much but now I have the worst cold any human being has ever had. I sneezed while brushing my teeth this morning and it took me fifteen minutes to find my toothbrush. Couldn't even make it in to the Owls Nest to have a game of smear this morning. I am just sitting here writing this with Vicks up my nose and feeling sorry for myself.

We hope to go to Wisconsin tomorrow to see our daughter, but we hear that they still have a foot of snow on the ground. We would like to see her, but I do not need to see more snow.

The geese are standing around on the ice on the lake, wondering why they can find no water. I believe that they are planning on starting their families, as it is about that time, even if the weather doesn't seem to want to cooperate.

Anyway, I am reasonably sure that by the time we set off the fireworks in Hancock on the Fourth of July, the car will have fallen through the ice on the Mill dam and the snow bank in our grove will have melted.

Clothing

Fashion Gets Closer to My Personal "Look"

Somewhere in this world there is a person, or maybe a committee that decides what is stylish and what is not. These people seem to change their minds occasionally, sometimes a lot, and when they do, people dress differently to please these arbiters of fashion. I am usually a little behind the current trends, but in the circles in which I rotate, it doesn't make much difference.

The last thing I heard is that the Western look is no longer in favor. You know, tight jeans, high-heeled boots, a bolo tie with a big purple stone on it, a shirt decorated with embroidery and a belt buckle the size of a Cadillac hubcap. A big hat, worn indoors as well as outside, tops the outfit.

They say that fashion has moved farther west and the lumberjack look is in. Loose pants, heavy boots, and a plaid shirt. They are getting a little closer to the Rasmusson look, and I appreciate it. When I was young, I wore Levis, but I was shaped differently then. Now I am built rather like a carrot, or maybe a rutabaga; anyway, the taper runs the wrong way for me to hold my pants up without suspenders. I have both styles of suspenders, the ones with elastic and the ones without, and have no opinion on which is the best as both have advantages.

Now I go all the way and buy overalls. I have striped ones, which I feel are somewhat slenderizing with the vertical pattern, and some nice conservative blue ones for more formal wear. They have plenty of pockets, a place for a pliers along the right leg, a loop for a hammer, and for those so inclined, a pocket for the snoose box on one's chest, up where it is not likely to be crushed.

For warm weather, I can unbutton the sides so a little air will circulate up the roomy pant legs and out the top, making me cool and comfortable. In cold weather there is room enough to wear another pair of pants inside for more insulation.

A friend has a pair of overalls with a zipper in the fly. This is not traditional. (I am tempted to say it flies in the face of tradition.) But I suppose I should not shut from my mind the possibility that improvements can still be made. After all, buttonholes wear out and can embarrass a person, and I have doubts about how Velcro would work.

Caps

I've been thinking about caps. I suppose it's because the weather has been getting a little warmer, and earflaps have not been as critical a need the last few days. So, I have been digging in my collection for an appropriate cap, one not too summery, but still lighter and more carefree than my big wool cap with the button on top.

This makes me think specifically about what are generally known as seed corn caps. I know many refer to them as baseball caps, but when did a ball club ever give anyone a cap? When I get something free, I give the givers the credit.

Not that seed corn people are the only people who give out the caps; a lot of manufacturers, and almost any enterprise around have their name on a cap nowadays. But around here seed corn and feed companies were the first to give away a lot of them. I have heard of people actually buying caps with logos on the front, but think it must be just an idle rumor.

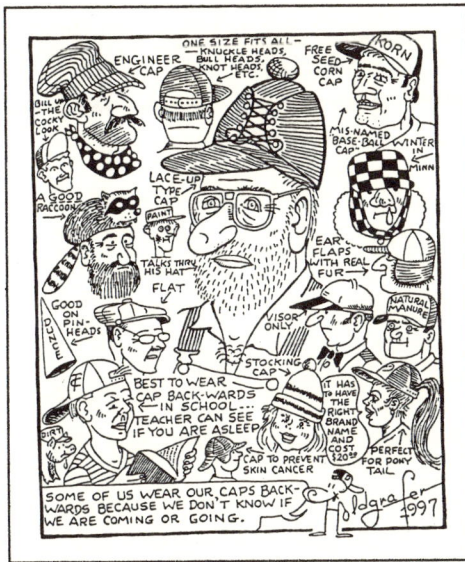

I remember when the cap industry first started to change. My dad got a cap from some hog feed company. The name on the cap was for a mineral that the salesman said was lacking in the soil around here, and just a smidgen of this stuff every day for your pigs would make them prosper, like the ones in Iowa. I don't know what he told the people in Iowa. The cap was not much, but it was vastly more valuable than the stuff it advertised.

The cap was made like one the railroad people used to wear in the summer time. It was constructed of a black and white striped material like that used in overalls, and was made with a high crown, kind of like a chef's cap, except that it had a visor. It had the name of the feed company painted on the front, and came in two sizes, way too big and way too small. Dad took a large size, and had to take a tuck in the back to keep it from falling down over his ears. The small one would hold maybe a pint, pint and a half, something like that.

Which reminds me, somewhere in the stuff I have managed to accumulate I have a winter railroad cap, black wool with a button on top and laces in front to adjust. One still sees this kind in use in winter. I think they are used for traditional reasons rather than practical ones. I remember trying to make this thing fit me, but I was never able to. I think you had to have special training, belong to the union, or have a head shaped differently from mine.

The cap industry really got started when someone invented the one-size-fits-all cap with the hole in the back and the plastic strap you can adjust. The hole is handy if you have a ponytail. Then you can thread the hair through the hole and the wind will never be able to blow your hat off. I, of course, have never had that much hair. Only the younger generation is able to make use of this feature.

Speaking of younger people, why, in the name of all that's reasonable, do they wear these caps backwards? I have asked some, and have never had a sensible explanation. Of course, that is not the only thing that young folks do that I fail to understand.

Use It All Up

Not so much anymore, but it used be a universal rule that nothing should be wasted. "Clean your plate! So what, you don't like your gruel, or your cold fried egg sandwich, or whatever, somewhere a child is starving, and would give anything for that bowl of slop." All us old folks heard that when we were growing up. "Use it up, wear it out, or learn to get along without." That's another one I heard quite a bit.

Suppose you were going to 4-H camp or going to stay overnight at a friend's, you had to find some socks and underwear that had no patches or darned spots. Sometimes that was not easy to do. I don't know why we bothered to do this; nobody else had much new stuff either.

I think the worst summer I ever put in was the year my Uncle Ross died. I inherited his shoes, and had to wear them out. This was all right in the spring, but this was the summer I did most of my growing, so for the last part of that summer I limped or went barefoot until school started. Then I was entitled to a new pair.

Cleanliness may be next to Godliness, but when I was young it was also next to impossible. My folks talked about how nice it was back when our lake had water in it. They said they would go for a swim every night in the summer time to wash off the dirt they had accumulated walking behind the horses all day. By the time I came along, the lake was as dry as banished hope. It didn't fill up again until I was married, but by this time we had a bathtub, and didn't really need the lake.

Getting back to this using up thing, a friend of mine was telling me about a conversation he had with his thirteen-year-old grandson. They had been working together getting the kid's dad's harvest completed, and the young guy said, "If you can hold out for another four or five years, grandpa, dad and I will have it made." Wear out the old first.

Clothes With a Message

I was reading a guy's shoes the other day. Easy to do. The printing was pretty big, and I had just gotten my new glasses. There was no real message on the shoes, just a bunch of numbers and a word "cross-trainers", whatever that means, and another word, probably a brand or the manufacturer's name. Same on both shoes. They missed a bet there; they could have had two different messages.

I guess most of these rubber and plastic shoes are made in China or somewhere on the Pacific Rim, but the names are in English anyway. What do they do with the ones they sell in Europe?

When I was young there was very little writing on clothes. A basketball shirt would have a number, and that was about it. The shirt seldom even had the name of the team on it. They must have figured you knew which side you were on.

The first place I saw a lot of printing on clothes was on seed corn caps. As long as you got the cap free, you felt it was all right to advertise a little for the company. And after you had leaned into the cow for a while milking, you couldn't tell what it said on the front of the cap anyway. Just kind of a hairy brown smear, but at least the stuff wasn't in your hair.

I see pictures of soldiers back in the old days, and other than different colors, and maybe more gold and silver braid on the big shots, there was no printing at all on their uniforms. I suppose most people couldn't read, but as they could tell colors, that was the way they told who was who. It's important to know who you're fighting. Nobody seems to care why, however.

Now everything has writing on it. Sweat shirts, T-shirts, coats, everything has stuff written all over it. Jeans have huge labels on the rear end. And I don't think we've seen the last of it yet.

When folks are married or buried, the clothes they wear are generally unmarked. Pretty soon, I'll bet brides will be buying wedding dresses that have the name of a sports team or a soft drink, or maybe a vacation place printed on the front and back. And they will gladly pay a little extra because of it.

Overalls

I know that bib overalls are not very stylish, but they are comfortable. Especially if your stomach is a little larger than average and your butt is smaller. This leaves you with nothing for the belt on ordinary pants to catch on, so you must resort to suspenders, another piece of equipment to purchase and worry about. They either button onto one's pants, if you have pants with buttons in the appropriate place, or clamp onto the waistband with some clips that are continually coming loose or coming apart, and requiring maintenance.

Louise says it happened at a cafe in Steele, but I believe it was in Jamestown, North Dakota. It was on a Sunday; Louise and I were travelling home from her brother's place in Rawson, and stopped for coffee. I was dressed uncomfortably in a pair of jeans, and was pulling them up as I walked into the café. I saw this fellow wearing a pair of overalls, complete with pliers pocket and hammer holster, but made out of a nice Harris tweed. Plenty good for church. I introduced myself and asked where he had found these wonderful things. He said that his wife had made them after he had complained long and loud about how tough it was to wear a suit after being dressed in comfort all week.

His wife was an accomplished seamstress, so she took a pair of his beloved bibbies and disassembled them so she could use the parts as a pattern and made him a pair out of some nice dark blue serge. He said people hardly noticed when he wore them to church the first time, as the suit coat covered the suspenders and the front part with all the pockets, so this gave the rest of the congregation a chance to adjust to his new appearance gradually.

He said his wife enjoyed the challenge, so now he has many pair, some in heavy wool for the cold weather, and some light-colored ones for summer wear.

They play in an occasional bridge tournament, and he was of the opinion that the overalls gave them a slight competitive advantage, maybe distracting the opponents. It would be kind of like playing tennis in black stockings.

Mankind is making some progress. Now if we can get rid of neckties.

Pants

I look with wonder at these young, modern farmers. The size of the investment they have to make boggles my mind. I am amazed at the long hours of hard work and the management ability they need to even partly succeed, compared to what they could probably do in some off-the-farm job or business, with an equal investment and management need, it makes me happy that I am only partly involved in agriculture. The decisions I have to make, the things that occupy my mind now are of a less critical nature. Here is an example.

I picked up a pair of overalls in town yesterday, and tomorrow I am going to take them back. I am somewhat embarrassed to say this, but I find that they are a little tight. At least tight enough to interfere with my comfort, and at this point in my life I will not put up with that. It may be just that it is a different brand, and they size them differently. We'll see.

I remember the first time I had to ask for size 40-waist pants. It was hard to do. Those small increases I could handle, I went 32, 34, 36, 38, no problem. But when you make the jump to 40 you start to wonder if you couldn't use a good diet or maybe a change in lifestyle, or perhaps some magic pill, anything that would slim one down a little. Or maybe a lot.

Maybe it would upset me less if they measured the diameter of pants instead of the circumference. They do it with hats. Let's see, 50 divided by 3.14, that would be about a size 16. I could live with that, I think it sounds a lot better.

Animals

54

Wood Ducks

We seem to be having a population explosion with the wood ducks here on the shores of Long Lake. There are some duck houses hanging on the cottonwoods along the east side, and they must be full, as now the ducks have moved into our yard and grove.

On Sunday, Louise, our daughter Andrea and I were watching two that seemed to be planning on setting up housekeeping in the old box elder east of our house. Mrs. Duck was trying desperately to get into a hole in the tree that was just a little too small for her. It seemed to me that she had eggs to lay, and was desperate. Her husband was pacing back and forth nervously on the lawn under the tree. I commented to the ladies about how worried and upset the husband seemed to be. The women disagreed.

The ladies said that, like a typical man at a time like this, he was not being the least bit useful. He could have been out checking locations himself, or at least standing on the limb alongside his wife with a beak full of nest building material. And, they said, he was not pacing nervously, he was just chasing and eating bugs on the lawn with the blackbirds. A typical male, turning over the bulk of family responsibilities to the woman. No real commitment, all he was interested in was his own satisfaction.

So while the three of us were watching the same thing, at the same time, we still got different ideas about what was going on. We could not agree on Mr. Duck's attitude, or his obligations.

Of course, Mr. Wood Duck is dressed a lot fancier than his wife, and maybe he just didn't want to get his nice feathers mussed up by trying to get into little holes in the tree. I notice that the geese seem to share housekeeping chores just about fifty-fifty, but then I can't tell the goose from the gander. But I assume they can, and that's all that is necessary.

Dinosaurs

Louise and I have been away from home for three days. The weather was beautiful, and with the sunshine, we noticed everything seems to have improved a lot around here in that short time.

We went to St. Peter to a church convention and slept in a dormitory for a couple of nights. The last time we were there it was hot, so this time we took a fan, which was not needed. While the weather was warm, it was not uncomfortably so.

The beds were the same, though, made for young people who do not have to get up at night, people for whom sleep comes easily and in most any circumstance.

I have a problem leaving home. It seems that things that work poorly for me at home, work hardly at all when I am away from home.

This makes me think about a thing I heard on the radio about dinosaurs and why they disappeared. They agreed a weather change was mainly responsible. One guy thought they had bad eyes, the sun got too bright, and they became blind and couldn't find food. Another thought that they became constipated when their diet had to change as the climate changed, and that killed them. I can go along with that last theory.

We shouldn't complain. They fed us well at the convention, maybe even a little too well. Being elderly, one is sometimes impatient, and if the proceedings had been on tape, I would have been tempted to push the "fast forward" button once in a while. But we heard some very good, informative talks, met many old friends we haven't seen in a while, and gathered a little information that we may be able to take back to our congregation if we can remember it.

A lot of printed material was given us, both before we went and at the meeting, but the volume of the stuff was so great I doubt if we can find what we are most interested in. So if we have to depend on memory, well, the mind doesn't work that well anymore either.

Where Are the Meadowlarks?

Chuck Myers mentioned to me yesterday that he has, of late, taken to sitting outside these nice evenings when the bugs aren't too bad and he wonders why he doesn't hear any meadowlarks. He hears the mourning doves, an occasional robin, and the twittering of other anonymous birds, but no meadowlarks.

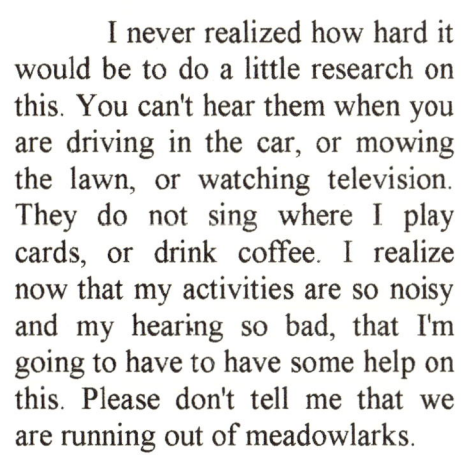

I never realized how hard it would be to do a little research on this. You can't hear them when you are driving in the car, or mowing the lawn, or watching television. They do not sing where I play cards, or drink coffee. I realize now that my activities are so noisy and my hearing so bad, that I'm going to have to have some help on this. Please don't tell me that we are running out of meadowlarks.

I've mentioned this to a few

people, and one fellow said he had heard one lately, but most hadn't or hadn't been paying any attention. Too many other things going on, so who worries about the meadowlarks?

We have geese nesting in the neighborhood, something that I do not remember when I was young. Pelicans are on our lake now, catching fish and floating around with great dignity, and then flying, gliding with the updrafts. An occasional coyote is seen, a new thing to me, and that's fine.

This time of year you can watch the martins and the swallows swooping around, catching bugs, or sitting on the wires resting, but that is a visual thing. You can do that when you are making noise.

Fixing fence, picking rocks or doing anything with horses out in the field you had opportunity to listen, but now you must make that opportunity. I hope it isn't too late.

More Birds

I'm always a little surprised when somebody tells me that they have read what I have written, and have thought enough about it so that they have formed an opinion.

Evidently many people have strong opinions about meadowlarks. A neighbor told me he has not heard a meadowlark for at least four years and accused me of not paying attention. I plead guilty to that and am ashamed.

Then, another regular coffee-drinker said that early Sunday mornings, before church, he will sometimes drive around out in the country, and he generally hears meadowlarks when he parks at the airport. Lots of short grass, just the environment that they need. Another called and said I would have to go west, out into the Dakotas where the grass is shorter to hear the birds.

While sleeping at my brother-in-law's place south of Williston, North Dakota, I generally hear coyotes. We are going out west, before Labor Day for a little while, and I intend to spend a lot of my time listening for other things. Now I suppose someone will tell it is too late in the season.

Another person confused meadowlarks with the killdeer. I remember when working in the fields with smaller, slower moving equipment, seeing the killdeer run ahead of the implement, dragging one wing, crying out plaintively, to draw you away from her primitive nest. Just three or four eggs in a little depression in the dirt, none of the amenities that other birds built for themselves to raise a family. It seems to me they would have had better luck saving their eggs if they would have stayed right by them and helped us find them, because we always tried to miss the nest if we could.

I am a little ashamed of my ignorance about some of these inedible flying things that we take so much for granted. I suppose things change, things come and go, and economic realities and Mother Nature cause this to happen. Just now a big doe and two fawns are standing on my lawn, real ones, not the concrete kind. When I was a kid, if someone went up north and shot a deer, they would haul it around on the fender of their car until they were sure all the neighbors had seen it.

Even More Birds

This bird thing is getting out of control. I'm going to have to find something else to write about. However, I now have good reliable information on meadowlarks. Rita Atwood writes from North Dakota that she has a lot of them at her place. They are the first to come in the spring, and don't leave until October. But she is short on killdeer.

We are not short on geese. It was a thrill for me a few years ago when they started nesting around here, and we would see them with their young parading around the edges of the lake. I have heard people complain, people who lived near the Lac Que Parle refuge, but I thought they were just people who would complain about anything. I heard people in some of the towns, like Fergus Falls and Rochester complain about them on their lawns and sidewalks, and on the golf courses, but I had no sympathy. I am a farmer and am used to a little manure on my shoes once in a while.

But now they are eating my renter's soybeans, and my hope is that part of those soybeans are mine, and I resent it Now, I think we have too many geese in Minnesota. Tonight, I visited with a former DNR employee, and he said he was glad he was retired, and did not have to listen to goose complaints. That's complaints about geese, not from geese. He said some of the wildlife people are starting to refer to them as "Sky Carp".

I guess it just goes to show that too much of anything is not good. Too many people in one place, too many geese, I have even heard it said that too much money can ruin a person. Which reminds me, I better go see what the Power Ball numbers are.

Fertility

I was driving across the grade on Long Lake this morning and a small, struggling hawk of some kind flew right over the hood of the car. It was having trouble gaining altitude because it was carrying a large, worried looking bullhead in its claws. The lake is teaming with life, weeds, various water bugs, algae of different kinds, minnows, and as you go higher on the food chain, bigger fish, pelicans, cormorants by the dozens, and finally a few fishermen.

We complain about our lakes, and I guess the reason we complain is because they have more life in them than we think should be there. We would like clear water, the right temperature for swimming and containing a large number of walleyes and northerns, but having no minnows, so the fish would be always hungry and our bait would look good to them.

This is not the way nature works, and maybe it is a good thing. I complain about large cities a lot. I say they are stinking masses of too much of everything. But maybe they are a little like our sloughs and shallow prairie lakes, teaming with life and fertility.

But there may be another similarity; we can improve our lakes and rivers with a little management. A little less soil washed into them, care in the spread of more foreign species, like zebra mussels, milfoil, carp, that sort of thing, and we can make our lakes better. Or at least slow their natural degradation. Somebody else will have to figure out what to do about Minneapolis and St. Paul.

Fishing

For a person who has lived most of his life by a lake, I am not much of a fisherman. Even when working out in North Dakota and Montana where I spent a good part of my time standing on bridges or wading in rivers, I did very little fishing. So what I know about the art is what I hear from others. Fishermen being what they are, I don't imagine my information is too accurate.

Howard is as close to an expert in the art as anyone, and he shared an experience with me the other day. Living in Hancock, he felt a responsibility to test Page Lake occasionally, even if the prospects for success were dim. The lake had yielded no fish for some years. It takes time and patience to do this properly, sitting on the rocks by the Cyrus-Hancock road, watching the bobber for signs of life. Patience is something that Howard has plenty of. You have to try it for at least two hours at a time, at different times of the day, over a period of days if you are going to learn anything.

He told me he was doing this some years ago and having no luck, when Albert stopped by. They visited a little, and Albert said he had a few crappies he had caught that morning up by Hoffman and didn't want to clean them, and wondered if he could put them in Howard's pail. He did and left.

Shortly thereafter, John stopped, silently looked into Howard's bucket, then got his pole out of his car, installed one of Howard's minnows on his hook and started to fish right beside Howard. They were both silent. Pretty soon another car stopped and joined in this exercise in futility. Howard was getting a little embarrassed and perhaps feeling a little guilty about misleading these people, so he packed up and moved over the Luthi's side of the lake. From there, he could see more cars stopping and a crowd gathering. He had no luck at his new location, either, so he packed up again and started for home. He had to pass by the now considerable crowd on his way, so thought he should stop and tell them the truth about the origin of the fish in his bucket.

Just as he stopped, John pulled out a crappie about three times the size of the ones Howard had been given. Everyone was catching fish, as fast as they could pull them in.

This is the way all great discoveries are made, by patiently waiting for an accident.

Ducks

I shouldn't believe everything people tell me, especially when the information would have no practical use, even if it were true. And when I do hear this kind of stuff, how come I remember it? I forget most of the important things.

Anyway, here is a method for catching ducks. A guy who many of you may know told it to me, and this does nothing for the credibility of the tale.

This system works, he says, because of the explosively fast digestion that ducks have. Anyone who has been around where ducks have been can verify that. And also the fact that they have a taste for fat, greasy things, and these things will pass through their bodies with even greater velocity than the things they normally eat.

So, he says, you tie a piece of raw bacon or something similar to a length of fish line, and tie the other end to a tree, or some solid object, something too large for the duck to swallow. The length of the line determines how many ducks you wish to catch, because the bacon passes through the ducks fast, with very little loss of quality, so another duck, and another and another will pick it up, eat it, and be caught.

Now I have never tried this, and have no intention of trying it, as I do not care that much for duck, but if someone else would care to experiment, I would appreciate hearing how well it works.

This is the same gentleman who once showed me his hammer, a very old one that had been in his family, he said, for several generations. Of course, he said, it sometimes required repair, as he himself had replaced the head three times, and put on many, many handles.

The Ocean

We here in Minnesota are about as far from the ocean as we can get. Some seem to think that because of this we have a great curiosity, a huge need to know about things oceanic. Have they ever thought that the reason we live here is because we like it here, about a thousand feet above the sea, safe from high tides, hurricanes and invading armies?

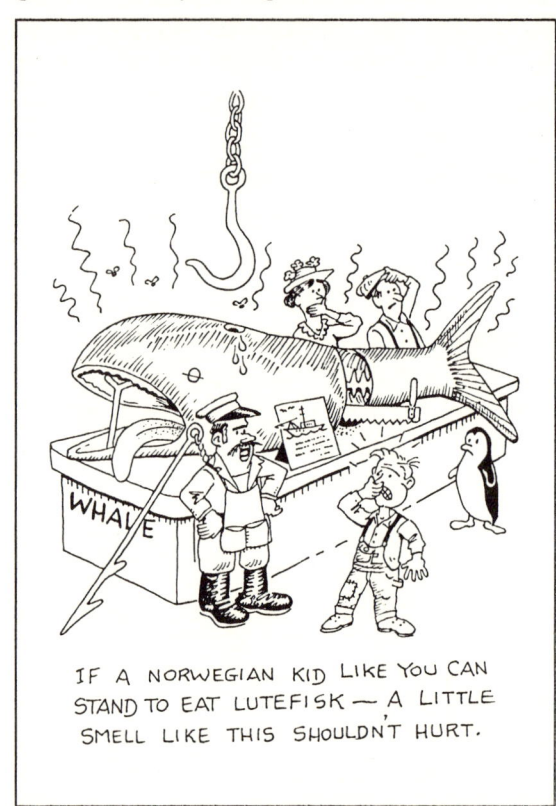

I am reminded of this because I heard on the radio that the folks who built the big aquarium in the Mall of America are a couple of payments behind on the twenty some million in bonds they sold to finance the thing. When you have seen one fish you have seen them all. That is my opinion, and it must be shared by a lot of others.

IF A NORWEGIAN KID LIKE YOU CAN STAND TO EAT LUTEFISK — A LITTLE SMELL LIKE THIS SHOULDN'T HURT.

Many years ago a whale came to Morris. It was dead, of course, very, very dead. Had been dead for quite some time. The people who brought it had made an attempt to embalm it but had been less than successful. The animal was in a boxcar with its mouth propped open and after paying your dime, you could walk around and look at it. I believe an octopus and some other lesser creatures of the sea were also scattered around for one's edification.

I was impressed mainly by the smell. If the E.P.A. and all the various other pollution control agencies would have been in existence then the beast would never have been allowed to leave the ocean. I was a farm youth accustomed to smelling dead things. I had cleaned the chicken house in the middle of the summer. Bad smells were nothing to me, I thought, but the dead whale was more than I could handle.

I suppose now that there are ways to irradiate or freeze big things from the ocean and bring them to us, but I say why bother. Unless it is something good to eat, just show us a picture. We don't have to touch it or smell it to know it is real.

Health

Smells

I think the clean, sharp smell of the cottonwoods along the lakeshore when they bud in the spring is wonderful. It makes up for the white fuzz they intend to spread over everything a little later in the season. Maybe I like it so much because it is the first of Mother Nature's natural perfumes that we encounter after a long winter of dry indoor heat and sinus problems. The lilacs, the honeysuckle and the smell of the cedars are maybe even nicer, and more obvious, but they come later, and we do not appreciate them quite as much.

I haven't smoked for about five years now, and I notice odors more. When I was consuming two or three packs of Merits a day it took a skunk under my car or a load of hog manure fresh from the pit to get my attention. Now I have a nose like a bloodhound. I am starting to recognize people by their aroma. Can't remember names, just smells.

I haven't yet mastered the dog's ability to be able to distinguish between various barely detectable odors, and still be able to bury its nose in some disgusting, rotten mess and enjoy it, as if it were a wonderful perfume. I expect, however, to someday achieve this ability. A smell will be neither bad nor good to me; it will just carry a message of some kind to my brain. Already the smell of lutefisk makes me hungry.

Of course, a few people use shaving lotions or colognes that make your eyes water, that may even sometimes trip the smoke alarm. Anyone can recognize them. This does not take a sophisticated nose like mine. I sometimes feel that I can distinguish between brands of toothpaste, even after the person has had breakfast. And when they walk by, I can tell if they have ridden in a new car lately. Of course, you who know me know I have a tendency to exaggerate, but you get the general idea.

It's hard for me to understand why, as I grow older, and my hearing fails, and my eyesight dims, and my step becomes as uncertain as my memory, that my nose should become more powerful.

Because the older I get, the worse I smell, and I have to live with it.

Walking

I've been watching people move about lately. I seem to spend more and more time stationary, so that gives me the opportunity to see the world go by. Not a lot of the world, as I travel little, but I feel enough so that it is a good cross section.

Everyone moves a little differently. How many times have you seen people, even from a great distance, and recognized them from the way they walk. I suppose that is why they have so many names for the various means of locomotion that we use.

My mother said that I crawled quite early. Slowly, I would imagine, at first, I suppose you could say I crept. then, a little faster, possibly scampered. The first steps, one toddles, trots, and maybe even a little more scampering.

There is an age when kids run a lot. Some, I see continue well into middle age, but I quit running quite early in life.

I have limped, doddered, paced, and once or twice, in an emergency, scrambled. To be honest, I can recall staggering once or twice. I have traipsed and I have trod. When feeling a little fancy, I have promenaded and perambulated. But I am more likely to trudge, slog, or plod along. I see people in a hurry, loping or trotting, and sometimes stumbling.

If one has no particular place to go and is in no hurry, you could saunter, or perhaps stroll. And if you speeded up just a little, you could amble.

Horses trot, canter, gallop, and with a lot of training, will pace. I think you need four legs to do the last two.

I believe that when I started this, there was a point I would like to have made, but it escapes me now. I was just carried away, and apologize.

The New Thumb

I was reminded of something I saw on the TV news the other day. I was sitting in the bathtub, and one gets a fairly good look at one's toes there. Without my glasses, mine don't look too bad, but they couldn't stand close inspection.

This young fellow on the news had lost his thumb in an accident, and the doctors had removed one of his big toes and made a new thumb out of it. It didn't look real good in the picture, but it had just been completed, the seams showed, and I suppose it was still swollen. But they said that as the toe is stronger than the thumb, he will have a powerful hand when he gets used to operating it.

Like I say, it didn't look very good, but it sure looked a lot better than one of mine would look.

You see, when I was about nine years old, I was attempting to harness a horse, and the animal stepped on one of my big toes. I was barefooted, the barn floor was concrete, and the horse had summer shoes on, so I have had no joint in that toe since.

Many years later I was helping move a refrigerator and it slipped off the dolly and landed on the other big toe, so that one now functions poorly.

Also, I have a fungus growing under the nails on my big toes, a yellow, miserable thing that causes the nails to become thick, wrinkled and ugly, and can be gotten rid of only by taking a powerful medicine for several years that gives one an upset stomach. The treatment is so unpleasant, I prefer to keep the fungus.

This man in the news was young, and his toes had not been through as much as mine, so I suppose it will work, but for me it is not an option.

But if it did become necessary, I would certainly lose weight. I can't imagine feeding myself, bringing that new thumb, stiff and yellow, holding a spoonful of food up by my mouth, well within range of my bifocals.

I'm Not Much Good Anymore

I've been told this on several occasions, and am starting to believe it. Constantly finding new things that I cannot do, or do wrong, or take too long to do, is not helpful to the ego.

I am sitting just a few feet from our new computer, which has me completely baffled. This one, our old one that we love and understand, has a hitch in its get-a-long and we have been assured that it is not to be depended on. I never expected to be a member of a two-computer family, and I take no pride in it. How can I, when one is reluctant to work, and the other one only confuses us.

We now have a mouse, not the furry kind, but one that moves a dot around on the screen so we can point to various little pictures that are called, for some reason, icons. My dictionary says that an icon is a sacred image, something that people worship.

Then, another word "defragmatize" is used, and that is a process, I understand, that may possibly give new life to this good old machine. It would put all the pieces of information now scattered about on our hard drive into one place, leaving vast open places for more of my crap. That "F" word would have to come, I believe, somewhere between deformity and defraud in my dictionary, and it is not there.

I hate to tell these computer people their business, but what about if they used a word like "consolidate" instead? I may be overly suspicious, but I think these companies enjoy confusing old folks.

But I intend to keep trying. For one reason, the printer works better, and then, we have a microphone attached to this new machine, and I understand it can learn to recognize our voice, and do what we tell it to do. Fortunately, this feature has not been activated yet, for I have told it some pretty unpleasant things.

Guarding One's Health

I bit into something hard about a year and a half ago and broke a chunk from one tooth. While it doesn't hurt, and I have grown accustomed to the roughness, I really should go to the dentist.

I received a letter a while back reminding me that it has been quite some time since I had an eye examination, and perhaps my glasses need changing, as eyes change with great age.

Then I went to the pharmacy to get another batch of the pills I require, and was told that my prescription was out of date. It has been a long time since I visited the doctor. I suppose it would be a good idea to find out if I am taking the right stuff, and if I need more or less of something.

So I decided to take these things in order. First, I will have a physical, to see if I am in good enough shape to make getting new glasses and having my teeth fixed worth while. I am in good enough shape so that I would not hesitate to buy green bananas, but one must be practical. After all, one does not buy a set of expensive tires for a car that has lots of miles on it and is using oil. When the motor is shot, a flat tire is the least of your worries.

I have started the process today. So far I have been shot in both arms, looked over and felt of, listened to, and been treated to the Vaseline and rubber glove treatment. I have a little less blood now, as they are examining some of mine.

I have been talked into having another examination with an instrument called a sigmoidoscope. I was given a paper that describes the process, and it says that one may be nervous and apprehensive. They are correct about that, but I trust my doctor. Whether I will after the procedure remains to be seen. I will, they say, hear noises made by the machinery that operates this thing, but that will not bother me, as I am a little hard of hearing. What I don't want to hear is someone saying "Whoops!"

Striving For Good Health

I've noticed that as I grow older medicine does not work quite as well as one expects it should. That was probably always the case, but when I was younger, I had other things to do that were more important than considering my various aches and pains. My daughter points out that it must work fairly well, as I am still alive, but I still would like something more.

In experimenting with various things to make me healthier, I have found a few things that have worked for me. They may work as well for others.

First, of course, was quitting my two or three pack a day smoking habit. It was a little late in life to quit. A lot of damage had been done in the forty years I smoked, but I'm sure quitting helped anyway.

When I smoked, I snored. In my youth, I slept on my back, but Louise forced me to sleep on my side, as this cut down the volume somewhat. I believe that the neighbors once considered getting an ordinance passed that I was not allowed to sleep on my back in the township. It was that bad. But now, hardly a whimper.

Then, there is the thing with warts. Everyone has had an experience with a stubborn wart that defied Compound W and the doctor's best efforts. I have discovered all you have to do is sell the wart. Warts are mostly psychological anyway, so if you sell them to a friend they will disappear in a matter of days. The price is not important, two bits will move any wart. The buyer has nothing to worry about. Warts are not that smart, they will get lost in the transfer most likely and will never be seen again. I've gotten rid of several that way.

Then there is that fungus under one's toenails. I have it and have learned to live with it as I thought that was the only thing to do. But then Cliff Olson, who is a great believer in vitamins, showed me a cure. Merely break open a vitamin E capsule two or three times a week and put the oil on the toenail. He said it worked for him, and now I have been doing it for a couple of weeks, and I am seeing about a quarter of an inch of healthy growth on the afflicted toenail, and I hope for a complete cure.

Hearing

I'm a little hard of hearing. I'll admit it, not that it would do me much good to try to conceal the fact. The blank look I give people when they mumble is a tip off.

I remember one time, I was riding in the back seat, Louise and her sister-in-law were in front, driving around out in North Dakota and discussing a recent wedding that had taken place in the community. It was a classy affair, and I heard Eunice describe the flowers and the dresses worn by the various participants and finally she said that they "had two trained bears." This got my attention, and I asked how they had kept the animals under control. She explained that she had said, "The bride had two train bearers."

Hearing aids have been mentioned, but I do not believe in them. I know too many people who have them, complain about them, or never wear them. In my mind they merely plug up the opening into one's head and further restrict your hearing, and give off strange squeaks and whistles occasionally.

Lately I have been seeing an ad for one that fits totally in your ear, and is so small as to be practically invisible. I think this is completely wrong. The only possible use for a hearing aid is to indicate to others that they should speak up. If you can't see it, what good is it?

Hiding any of your afflictions is pointless. I wear glasses and am not ashamed of the fact that I need them. I will not struggle with contact lenses just for the sake of vanity. I am not ashamed of the fact that I need to have people speak up, and can see no reason for others to be embarrassed by it.

I guess it all boils down to vanity. I suppose I am as guilty as anyone. Before I came to my senses and started to spend most of my time in overalls, I wore jeans. I would not admit that my circumference had increased to a point where I could no longer wear my usual size. As the diameter of the hips does not increase as fast as the waist, I could continue wearing the same size pants as long as I wore them lower. But there is a limit as to how low one can wear one's pants, and modesty and the good wife forced me into overalls. And I am glad.

Exercise

I've never had any sympathy for people who complained of boredom. I've never been really sure of what it was like to be bored, that is, until now. Really, no matter what a person is doing, I figured that they should be able to occupy their mind with something, find something interesting about what they had to do, or where they were.

But then we got an exercise bicycle. Actually we've had it quite a while, got it right after my heart attack. The doc told me I needed some exercise, a little at first, and then a little more, as I got my strength back. Weather in Minnesota is not always the best for walking outdoors, so the bike would be an acceptable way to measure how much I was exerting myself.

I was never diligent with the machine. At first, it was interesting, one could put batteries in it, and hook a thing onto your ear lobe, and it would tell you how fast your heart was beating and how many miles an hour you were making. But even this moderate excitement got old pretty quickly. I tried putting it in front of the television, thinking that would entertain me while I pedaled. It was a failure, so we moved it to the basement where it was cool, and one could use it without bothering anyone else. Out of sight, out of mind. Then out of guilt, I suppose, we brought it back upstairs. So, for quite a while now, we have been walking around the thing, feeling guilty about not using it.

But now the doctor has shamed me into doing something about my weight. I hate exercise, just for exercise's sake. I was taught as a child that when you expend effort, you should be accomplishing something. Riding that bike numbs the mind and destroys any chance of creative thought. You are going no place, the scenery never changes, and the improvements in your physical condition come so slowly, if at all, that it feels like a waste of time.

I am not ashamed of feeling this way now, because I went to the Hancock Firemen's auction today, and now I know for a fact many others share this viewpoint. Most of the donations on the sale were things that were used, or slightly out of date, or needed some repair, but all the exercise bikes, rowing machines, weight benches, goofy little trampolines, and various other torture devices looked as good as new.

Now that I have the bike upstairs, I have put new batteries in the speedometer, and am going to grit my teeth and ride that sucker.

Interdependence

A combination of things caused this. First, an article in the National Geographic about the brain, and how they suspect that the chemicals that trigger memories and cause the body to respond may come from various far-flung places on the body, and travel in unusual ways to get to the brain.

Acupunture, the ancient Chinese remedy may, the author speculates, use the blocking of these pathways to help various things. It seems to work, sending signals to the afflicted part to stop the pain or even in some instances, to heal.

Then, it's fall and football is upon us. This is a game I played in my youth, a painful game, and my right hip hurts when I think about it, and so I am inspired.

The foot, to kick, must have a leg

to swing it through the air.
To function well, the leg in turn
must be one of a pair.
Between the legs, suspended,
are what they need to procreate.
And just above, the belly
holds the things the mouth has ate.
Now, these guts will furnish energy
to drive the whole machine,
The spine, the bones and muscles,
and all the glands stuffed in between.
These glands make potent chemicals,
that when they reach the brain,
cause thoughts that call for actions,
and may even cause us to refrain
from doing things we like to do,
as those acts may cause us pain.

Earwax

I was listening to a Chicago radio station the other morning, and it was announced that the first baby of the year for 1996 had been born eight seconds after midnight, and the first murder in the city had not taken place until nearly ten minutes later. I suppose you could call that progress.

But that is neither here nor there. Out here in the hinterlands our life is more secure and we can think about other things.

I may have mentioned that my son loaned me his electric nose hair clipper, a scientific breakthrough I have long awaited. When one's hands tremble, a scissors is dangerous, and while I have another implement, a sort of circular device that you insert in each nostril and then rotate the center part, it does not cut the hair. It only wedges it in so when you remove the machine, the hair comes, but by the roots, and your eyes water for some time.

And then we learned of another new device. Ear wax candles. I believe they said they are a Chinese invention. These are not candles made of earwax; they are candles made for the express purpose of removing earwax.

The people who told me about this are Norwegian and Republican, so I had to believe them. Anyway, you put the base of this hollow candle in your ear, have a friend light it, and as it burns the earwax is sucked up into the center of the candle. It is suggested you have someone standing by with a bucket of water or a fire extinguisher. I have purchased some of the candles, so in a little while I will be able to hear a pin drop.

Old Geezers

For some time now I have considered myself and most of my friends "old geezers." I hear the word used frequently to describe us, and it doesn't bother me. I kind of consider it a compliment. It means that we persist, we have taken everything that life and the elements have thrown at us and are still here, and while we are not exactly thriving, we are surviving.

When I have coffee most mornings, I have it at the "old geezer" table in any cafe I happen to be in. That is where all the knowledge resides, so it is where one can add to one's own knowledge, and correct some of the wrong ideas others may have.

Then I looked "geezer" up in the dictionary and discovered that Webster must be wrong. They try to tell me that it means an "eccentric man, or rarely a woman." While that is not as bad as "geek", which they say is a "performer of strange and depraved acts," it still is not the way I feel we should be described. I'll go along with the "old" but we aren't much weirder than the rest of the population.

Who died and made Webster king anyway? I think that we have the right to attach any meaning we want to a word. The medical profession does it, the computer people do it, and if they have the right to confuse people, so have we.

So I think that "geezer" should be a compliment. We will say it means "an important person, one to be listened to and accorded respect." Isn't that better?

A lot of words can't be defined anyway. Take "twinkle" for example. They say folks have a twinkle in their eye. Have you ever seen an eye twinkle? Stars twinkle, eyes don't. Eyes water, get bloodshot, but they never twinkle.

I just happened to think of that, and had to throw it in.

Geezerhood

I was listening to Garrison Keillor this weekend, and in his usual sermon about the natives from Lake Wobegon, he hit on something that was a little too close to home for me.

He talked about old geezers, and that pretty much takes in me and most of my friends. I suppose he is approaching geezerhood himself, so he thinks about this a little more now.

Anyway, the guy he was talking about had started, in his mature years, taking some pills, hormones or some such. He felt this medicine was making a considerable improvement in his short term memory, his energy level, and was even helping him lose a little weight. And not only that, but something seemed to make him feel a little more romantic, a feeling that his wife did not seem to share. Garrison did not mention if she was taking any pills. This was causing a little problem in their home, a little tension, and Garrison thinks he should stop taking the pills.

Garrison says that medicating one's self to avoid old age and its infirmities goes against nature. One should accept geezerhood gracefully. We are born, we mature, we raise our families, and then we should get out of the way for the good of the species. We have made our contribution, or at least have had the opportunity to make it, and now it is time to turn everything over to those who follow, who can build on the foundations we have put together.

Well, I'm convinced. I have heard of medicine that is rumored to help stop and even reverse the aging process, but I am never going to take it. If I were better at what I do, and if I had more energy, I would have to assume more responsibilities, I would have to work. I would miss out on a lot of card games, people would expect more of me, I would feel guilty about not keeping up, would be depressed, and would have to take Prozac.

Cosmetic Surgery

I'm getting entirely too much of my information from television. I try to avoid it, but it's too easy. You just sit there, kind of in a fog, and nothing good is on, but you watch it anyway, and it kind of soaks in.

Like today. I had been mowing the grass and came in to get cool and more or less automatically grabbed the remote control and turned the TV on. Some blonde lady with a talk show was interviewing people who had had a lot of cosmetic surgery. The first lady was 41, looked 20, and had spent $100,000 on face lifts, liposuction, implants of various kinds, and had even had her jaw sawed off and screwed back on in a slightly different configuration. Chemical peels, wrinkle removal, having fat sucked out of one place and installed somewhere else was an everyday thing with her. They showed a "before" picture of her, a normal enough girl, attractive, but not spectacular.

This lady and the next one interviewed excused this activity by saying it made them feel better. They had more active social lives, that is, when they were not in the hospital, and were able to date guys that were just as handsome and stupidly superficial as themselves. The hostess of this show had a whole row of these crazies to talk to, but I left to mow more grass.

It reminds me of an ad someone showed me in the Minneapolis paper some time ago. It was from a cosmetic surgeon, and he was interested in improving men, by adding to, by rebuilding, I don't know how to say this delicately, anyway he would enlarge something that is generally not seen. He said he had 6000 successful patients. I suppose they are all dating surgically altered ladies.

And then, last week, an attorney had an ad in the paper, offering to sue if you were a man who had had surgery of this kind and were not satisfied. He mentioned infection, failure to function, general dissatisfaction, and that he would get you big bucks.

It's a strange world out there.

Shopping

I am a Norwegian and Lutheran, so naturally I always expect the worst. And now that I am approaching my 70th year, and feeling its effects, I worry about how much worse it is going to get.

Things that used to work, now work poorly or not at all, or hurt when one tries to make them work. So, I speculate on how much worse it will be, and what is the worst possible combination of circumstances that might come to pass.

Memories fade, one forgets names, dates, things to do, but it could be worse. Some things need forgetting. Appearance deteriorates, but that's OK, I never was that beautiful anyway.

Your get up and go has got up and left. You see things that need doing, and mean to do them, but low energy levels hold you back, and the projects seem to pile up, but pretty soon you say to heck with it, and start a new list.

But today I went shopping with Louise, and found out the worst, the absolute worst way to end up. That would be as a welcome person at Wal-Mart, wearing comfortable shoes, a silly sleeveless kind of shirt with a large yellow smiling face on the back, pushing shopping carts out of the way and grinning at the customers, who, for the most part, ignore you.

If you should ever go to a Wal-Mart store the first thing you'll encounter as you enter in the door is the guy they call the greeter, he'll give you a big HELLO! It makes you think, "I wonder, is this someone I know?" But when you try to talk to him he's already turned away, more people coming through the door, so greetings he'll convey to each and every customer, but most pay no attention, or just give him a look of complete incomprehension. I wonder what his function is; does he really make things better? Or is he just inside the store to get out of the weather.

My Head Cold

I've found that I must not assume
that flu shots will make me immune
to bugs that get up in my nose
and make it run just like a hose.
My throat is sore, my body aches,
I wait until the fever breaks.

Couldn't sleep the other night, my sinuses were full and painful, so between shoving Vicks up my nose and coughing, I listened to the radio just about all night long.

Minnesota Public Radio goes into a lot of detail in the middle of the night, and they mentioned a lot of the trouble in the world that we don't ordinarily hear about.

I found that the Flemish people have a separatist movement, they want to get loose from Belgium. It makes me wonder, if they get their own country, would they call it Phlegm? Probably not.

Then they talked about another thing, the flower gardens in Toronto, Canada. I guess that they are very nice, with little bridges, fountains and waterfalls, and a few swans floating around amongst the lily pads in the ponds. A big metropolitan area can afford this type of thing. We can't do it here in our little town; it is beyond our means.

This luxury has a down side. Because it is a beautiful place, wedding parties like to have pictures taken here, and in periods in the summer when the flowers are at their best a lot of wedding parties come. They are generally on a tight schedule, have had perhaps a little too much wine, and they get into fist fights over who is going to be first and take advantage of the best light. This gives the police another job, keeping peace among the bridegrooms. This will never happen in our little town. I hope.

Even the animals are having trouble. They said that someplace in Africa they began to find an occasional dead rhinoceros. They hadn't been shot or poisoned, it looked like they had been trampled to death. Busted ribs, that sort of thing. This is not easy to do with an animal as powerful and tough as the rhino. But finally they got lucky; a game warden in a plane saw three young elephants attacking a rhino. They decided that they were adolescent elephants, teenagers, so to speak, that had lost their parents at too young an age, and were emotionally unstable. They were forced to shoot them. Another problem we will not be forced to deal with here.

Opinions

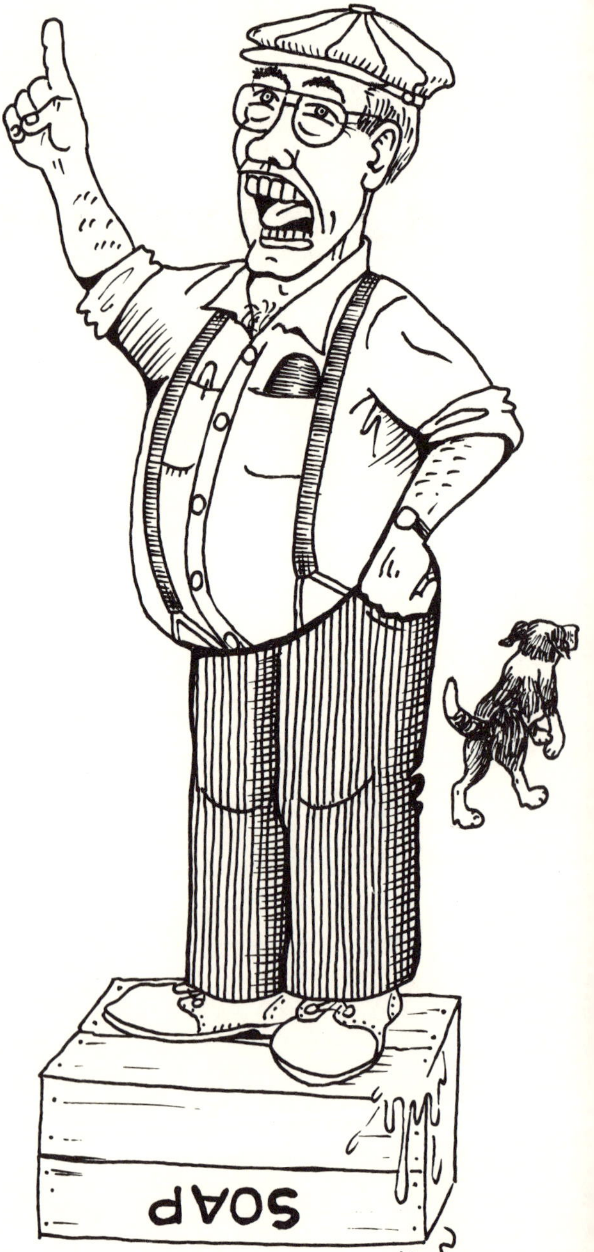
SOAP

The Bridges of Madison County

Louise didn't seem to be able to put the little book down. Then, after she had finished it, she seemed a little dreamy, kind of like she was in another world. She kept looking down the driveway as if she expected company.

Since I was a little curious, I read the book. It wasn't really about bridges so much as about this forty-five-year-old farm wife, an Italian war bride, who has an affair with a photographer. This takes place while her husband and kids are at the state fair for four days.

This guy is a handsome, artistic, Camel-smoking, Red-Wing-boot-wearing, flat bellied, hard muscled, vegetarian, picture taking, fifty-two-year-old with long silver hair, orange suspenders and an old pickup who works for National Geographic magazine. Hope I haven't forgotten anything. Anyway, he is an artistic guy, and the gal's husband is a farmer, so there you go.

They meet when he asks directions, and she hangs a note on the bridge he is going to take a picture of inviting him to supper, as she is a little lonesome.

He gets her started smoking again, and they do other stuff, but then they go their separate ways so as not to hurt anyone else.

After a long and happy life, her husband croaks. She tries unsuccessfully to find the Camel-smoking, Red-Wing-boot wearing, etc. and fails. He dies and she gets his cameras and stuff in the mail from the executor of his estate. Also his ashes are already spread on the bridge that she had hung the note on. She saves all his things, dies, and her kids find the stuff with the original note and a letter in a box hidden in her closet.

They take the news that mama had an affair pretty well. They realize that she was Italian, a little more hot-blooded than your average northern European, so you must allow for that.

One day is the longest I have ever spent at the State Fair since we've been married and Louise was along. And she isn't Italian.

County Roads

I have found something else to complain about, good roads. In my lifetime, the county roads here in Minnesota have been made wider, they have been hard surfaced, and they have been improved to the extent that they are better than a lot of the major highways. Louise and I had occasion to go north on #29 as far as #210 and then east to Hewitt. It was one continuous chuckhole. So when we returned home, we went on county roads, the traffic was lighter, the road smoother, and it made the trip a lot more pleasant.

You may ask why I would complain. Well, it is my nature to find things wrong with most everything, so I will complain about the system they use to number the county roads.

One goes from Highway #71 at Bertha west on county road #24, but when you leave Todd county you find you are on #40. This confuses me.

Closer to home, I live on Stevens County road #10, but when I go further east, I find that when I enter Pope County I am on Pope County road #18. If I would choose to go north from home, on Stevens County road #1, on entering Grant County I discover I am on #5, still a fine road, but on leaving Grant, I would be on a road not headed north, but one going east, finally to expire amongst the lakes in Ottertail County.

Ottertail and Todd counties each have a #73 running north and south, just a short distance apart. Both blacktop, smooth and straight, ready to confuse the unwary.

But then, maybe the various county commissioners, in their wisdom, have done this on purpose, created a system that only the local people will use. Then these wonderful roads will be saved and we will keep the tourists and all other occasional travelers out of the way, bumping along on the main highways.

How to Operate a Computer

If you are interested in learning to run a computer, there are a couple of things you must avoid. Pay no attention to books that say they will help you, because they will not, and do not listen to experts. Oh, they may help if you are young and speak the language of the young, but if you are my age, forget it. Watching and experimenting are the only way to learn.

Of course, you must have access to a computer. Our first one was a primitive model. I believe it had been built to operate on kerosene, and had been converted to electricity. It had no hard drive, so every time you turned it on, it was being reborn, and remembered nothing about its past life. But this was all right because everything you wanted it to know, and everything that you did, was on floppy discs that you put into the machine, and could take out again.

You will find that computers are fussy about the quality of electricity you feed them. They like to be turned on and off in a certain manner, and will destroy your data if you do either incorrectly. So find a young person, and have him or her turn it on and off a few times and watch carefully. Pay no attention to what is said, as they speak a different language than you do, but watch their fingers, and remember how it is done. It helps if you can get your young friend to do it slowly.

Our present computer is plugged into some sort of an electric strainer, something that takes out the lumps and clots from the current. These are caused by lightning and a mean streak that the power company seems to have. It has a switch and a little red light on it. So we leave the computer switches on all the time, and shut it off with the switch on this strainer, so we have a little less that we have to know.

If you buy a computer, the sales person will tell you of all the things it can do. Let your mind wander while you are being told this, as you do not need to know these things. In fact, it may be dangerous information. Think only of what you want it to do, and insist that these are the only things you want it to do. Otherwise, you will be playing games and looking for things the rest of your life, and never accomplish what you wanted the computer for in the first place. We old folks have limited time remaining here on earth, and we must be careful with it.

White Castle

Eating has always been important to me. Lately I have been more or less in charge of the cooking since Louise broke her ankle. This has made me pay attention even more. Funny how it works. I thought I had things pretty well in order, and then JoAnn Anderson came out and made us some brownies, and after she was finished, the kitchen looked and smelled a lot better than it does when I finish a project.

I just discovered that Shirley Swenson had fixed a little care package for us, some soup and a couple of bran muffins, but they never got here. Found out later that her husband ate them.

Our youngest son brought us something the other day that I didn't think existed, microwaveable White Castle Hamburgers. You older folks remember those little square vulcanized pieces of ground something? When I was young they were a dollar for a dozen in the cities. Even my grandfather, the most frugal man who ever lived, would not eat them. He tried one once; he had bought them because he couldn't resist the price. I believe it was the only thing he ever threw away in his entire life.

Anyway, that gets me thinking about how new inventions can affect things that have been around for a while. Some of the effects are good. For instance, vaccines have eliminated smallpox and polio pretty much. Coffee has been around for a long time, but I think that these automatic coffee makers are a big improvement. I like to read, and electric lights are a big improvement over the old Aladdin lamp with its mantle that was always getting smoked up or having a hole burned in it.

But then we have things like the White Castle burgers. They were bad, and science has made them worse. We could put up with Rush Limbaugh if nobody had invented the radio. Richard Simmons, that nut in the baggy shorts that wants everyone to kill themselves exercising, we could stand him if we didn't have television. Without television the infomercial would not exist, so you can see how it goes. It all fits together, warfare, the atomic bomb, and White Castle burgers.

The Bell Ringers

When music is being made by bell choirs, bagpipes or by people yodeling, I can tell right away. I'm not much at identifying musical stuff, but those three I can pick up on pretty quick.

The bells must be getting popular for some reason. I have run into two of them in the last few days. Not actually run into them, you understand, just been where they were performing.

You are all, I suppose, familiar with bell ringers, as you all get around more than I do. You know, it's a bunch of people with bright, shiny hand bells of various sizes playing tunes. The participants wear white gloves, I suppose so they don't leave their fingerprints on the shiny parts, and stand behind a cloth-covered table that has all these bells arranged on it.

They stand poised and ready to grab the appropriate bell when the music calls for it. They can make one of three tones, either a ding, a dingaling, or a melodious clunk. Of course, higher or lower pitched according to how big the bell is, and what is appropriate at the time. This takes quite a bunch of people, and they have to be well coordinated, everyone taking their turn to ding, dingaling, or clunk, according to what the music calls for.

I think that if people can train themselves to do this, work so flawlessly together, then the human race must be indeed capable of great things. They have, as I see it, only one failing. It seems that once they get started they can't seem to stop. They go on and on, until everything in the room is vibrating.

It could be worse, though. I suppose they could all start yodeling while they are ringing their bells.

Traveling

It makes about as much sense as the ordinary necktie, but I heard on the radio that the king of Thailand received one from an admirer. In honor of the king's fifty-year reign this guy had made him, out of 600 pounds of polyester cloth, a necktie twenty feet wide and over three hundred feet long. They didn't think he would ever wear it.

Now I will never get to see this necktie unless they haul it to Hancock, an unlikely happening. That is because I never go anyplace much. Certainly not to Thailand. I have been accused of believing that the earth is flat, and places like Thailand are over the edge. This is not true. I just think that everything I need is here, or will come here if one is patient.

Louise's sister Jean is not of that opinion. She has been on numerous trips to exotic places, like Norway, the center of the universe, and other places in Europe, and is now planning on going to Tanzania, in Africa. She stopped in the other day, both arms covered with those little bulls-eye Band-Aids on the places where she had received the series of shots needed to go to this place. If she survives these, they will give her the rest. If she still lives after that she will be given a bunch of pills to be taken daily for two weeks before going, while in Africa, and for two weeks after returning.

As I am planning on going to the west end of the county later this week, I intend to check with my doctor and see if I need to be vaccinated.

Air Bags

It seems as though the government does more harm than good when it mandates things, when it tries making things safer for us.

Air bags, for instance. Not the politicians. I mean the kind of air bags you find in cars. I hear on the news that 24 children and 12 adults have been killed this year by the things. I believe it, because I have seen what one did to the face of a friend of mine.

When you hit a deer, it is generally quite bad for the deer, and most of the time reasonably bad for the car, but the people in the car do not suffer. We have hit several deer, and while it averaged about $1800 to fix the car each time, and the deer died, we didn't get a scratch.

But my friend hit a deer, and the bag hit him in the face. I understand they inflate at 200 miles an hour. The bag, he said, is made of a fairly sturdy material, somewhat tougher than his nose and chin. The air bag is not designed to be reused, one shot, that's it. Your face, however, you like to use as long as possible. My friend is healed up now, and has a new bag installed in his car, but I doubt that when he trades he will get that option, if he can avoid it.

On a newscast I listened to, they said that now the government is going to insist that the manufacturers make a kinder, gentler air bag, one that, while it will keep you from going through the windshield, will not propel you violently into the back seat. Kind of a happy medium. Of course, this may raise the price of the new car, but so what. I can't afford one now anyway.

Center of the World

There is a map of the world hanging on the wall in the cafe in Hancock, next to one of Minnesota. It is a large map, so many details can be noted. People who have been around, who have traveled extensively, sometimes point out places they have been on this map, and give accounts of their adventures.

Like I say, it is a large map, and a little unusual in that the mapmakers have made it perfectly accurate. The maker has located Stevens County right in the middle, in the dead center of the known world. We have Europe and Africa to our right, the Pacific Rim and Asia to our left, Canada and the Arctic to the top of the map, and South America and the Antarctic below.

I am not too surprised to see this, and have known for some time that this is the place to be, but I didn't know it was common knowledge. One always hears about places like New York or Los Angeles being where the action is, where everyone must go at some time in their lives, but they are actually on the outskirts.

I am a little surprised that the traffic isn't worse here. One would think that if people have to go from one place to another, they would have to pass through this central location more often. They must take alternate routes and I am thankful for that. It is nice to drive up to a stop sign, look right and left, and see nothing coming clear to the horizon in either direction.

Driving along Highway #2 and passing through Rugby, North Dakota, you will see a stone monument with an inscription indicating that you are now at the geographical center of North America. This is all very fine, but I think it is much better to be the center of the whole world. They couldn't have picked a better place.

Loss of Appetite

Like a lot of people with a weight problem, I'm always looking for an easy, painless way of curbing my appetite. Our driveway is ready for another coat of gravel. This gets a little complicated now, so I hope you can follow me on this.

Anyway, I knew that the township was going to gravel some of the township roads this summer, and I wanted to hire whoever has the contract to put a little on my driveway and yard. In order to find out who had the job, I called one of the town board members, as these people know everything. Well, Erwin wasn't home; his wife Jean answered the phone. We visited for a while, and as I have one of those walk-around telephones, I was making a sandwich at the same time. I generally don't do two things at once, unless it has something to do with food. I can eat and do anything, except maybe sleep.

Now here is where this new method of appetite control comes in. Jean had been reading a book, and like anyone, when something makes a big impression on her, she wants to talk about it. You can understand that, can't you? The book was about Ed Geen. I'm not sure of the spelling, he was that fellow in Wisconsin who had a habit of digging people up out of the cemetery and eating parts of them. They caught him after he murdered a lady in a local hardware store. The book was complete with pictures, and Jean's description was enough to put off my sandwich building for a good long time.

I've still got to see somebody about hauling gravel.

Ethnic Food

This is liable to be a little longer than my regular epistles, as it is about food. This is a subject over which I am interested, because eating is something I can still do quite well, so I am likely to get a little long winded. We all know that America is a melting pot, we eat food from all over the world, and it shows. I'm pretty sure we are on average the fattest nationality, but it is nice to have such a wide variety of foods.

I had a meal once in an Irish restaurant, up in northern Minnesota, and I can see why the Irish emigrated. That famine they talk about wasn't from the potato blight, it was because the cooking was so bad nobody could eat it.

We stopped once at a Polish place over in northern Wisconsin. Really nice building, lots of logs and a big stone fireplace. The waiters wore funny hats with feathers and leather shorts. Really ethnic, I suppose. They advertised genuine Polish sausage, and if these were the real things, I'm glad we have only the imitation available around here. I am quite fond of the Polish sausages that are made by people in ordinary clothes but these things were long, skinny and black swimming in melted lard, just to look at them would plug up a couple of arteries.

French cooking varies from the good to the absolutely inedible. People refer to limburger from Germany and gammelost from Norway as strong cheese, but the French have a kind, I forget the name, that is so close to toxic I believe you have to sign a disclaimer of liability before they will sell it to you. I have never eaten any, but was near a piece once and my eyes water just thinking about it. Smelled kind of like ammonia, only with a trace of dead sheep.

Speaking of sheep, the Scots eat a lot of the parts of sheep that no one else will. They have that good whisky that makes everything look and taste different than it really is.

We had a meal in Winnipeg some years ago, in the Provender room of the Fort Garry hotel. Very fancy place, with a big menu. I was feeling adventurous and ordered steak and kidney pie. Figured if I couldn't handle the kidney part I could at least make out with just the steak and vegetables. Now, I assume that the cook knew what he was doing, everything else on the menu was just fine, according to the people I was with, but those kidneys made everything taste kidney, even for a couple of days after I got home. So much for English cooking.

Of course, if one has to settle on a menu from one country, it would have to be Norwegian. Klub, the white variety, made without the pig blood, is delicious. Or if you prefer, with the blood, if you want more protein. And either way you want it bathed with grease from the salt pork you have with it. This is a nourishing, satisfying meal. And then the next day, if you have any left over, you cut it into little chunks and warm it up in the frying pan with heavy cream. It's even better then. You may die a little sooner, but you will be happy.

And then of course the fish. We Norse do not eat them just as they come from the water. We dry them and soak them in lye, or pickle them, or if they are small, we can them in mustard or tomato sauce. This is completely different than the Japanese, who eat raw fish, some varieties that, if prepared incorrectly, will kill you instantly. Lutefisk will never do that.

The Norwegians know that potatoes are to be boiled, ground, mixed with flour and cream and then fried in thin sheets. This must be done carefully, so it remains flexible enough so it can be used to wrap around things that you eat. Originally it was intended to hold the lutefisk together when it was too slimy to stay on the fork, but it works for other things too.

Anyway, I am glad we have a choice here, even if it does make us a little on the fat order.

The Best Place To Live

I have no idea who these people are, or why their opinion is worth anything, but anyway, I read that they have published a new list of the best places to live in the U.S. I was somewhat surprised to see that Madison, Wisconsin was selected as the best. Number two and three were Punta Gorda, Florida and Rochester, Minnesota. The Twin Cities were 87th; no surprise there, in spite of the fact that I have heard claims that the Mall of America is the prime tourist attraction in this country. More so since they installed an aquarium with a tunnel through it so you can see the fish from the bottom. I fail to see the advantage in this. I have not been there, and have no intention of going just so I can see fish bellies.

I suppose they are vainly trying to come up with something in the class of Hancock's 4th of July celebration, or Donnelly's Threshing Bee, or Morris' Prairie Pioneer Days, or the Herman Iron Pour, or their bachelor surplus problem. Hancock was not on the list I saw. Neither was Morris, or even Herman. But that's OK. Let the true story be our little secret.

I am not much of a traveler, but oddly enough, the three top ones are towns where I have been. While I have not investigated them as well as I have Hancock, Morris, and surrounding towns, I feel I am still entitled to an opinion.

Louise had two uncles in Madison, Wisconsin. They lived in nice neighborhoods, by lakes, and spent a good share of their free time washing goose poop from their sidewalks. This does not happen here, or at least very seldom.

You should try Punta Gorda, Florida in an Avis rental car that has something wrong with its air conditioning. This was in late March, what do people do there in the summer?

Rochester, Minnesota is fine if you are sick, but I would rather not be sick. Can you blame me for this? I have never been there sick, just for conventions and such, and while it is OK, so are a lot of other places.

So I intend to remain here as long as I can. We have bugs, but I have been places where they have worse bugs. It gets cold here, but most of us have central heat. Rochester has a better hospital, but if worst comes to worst, the helicopter can get me there in jig time. I know a lot of people here, we have friends here, and I think that this is the best amenity of them all.

Caucuses

I didn't attend a caucus this year. I justify my not going a couple of ways, because when I have gone, I didn't feel that enough of my friends and neighbors were there to truly represent our community, and besides the weather was not as nice as it could be. It was snowing and windy. I have talked to some of my friends, and have found no one who did attend. I guess that means we are left out of a good part of the democratic process. When November comes, and I vote, I may not have the name on the ballot that I want to vote for, and it will be my fault. So I better not complain about it. But then, I have been to caucuses before, and have seen many strange things happen. I can accept this, because for some reason, our country seems to be able to stand this.

The system seems to work, but I can not for the life of me understand how. Not that it will ever happen, but I would like to propose an alternate system, one that would be easier on the eardrums, and not be such an embarrassment to humanity in general.

Maybe we could select office holders like we select jury members. Names would be randomly selected from the voter registration list, people would get letters telling them they had been chosen for high office, and unless they could prove hardship, or were ill, demented, or in jail, they would be sent to Washington, paid fifteen dollars a day and board, and be expected to do their civic duty until replaced.

Like a jury, they would be isolated from all outside influences, taking with them to our Capitol only what they knew of conditions back home. They would not be selected because they could talk louder, or had more money, or looked better on television, only because they thought enough about their country that they had at one time registered and voted, and did not try too hard to lie their way out of doing their duty.

But then, on second thought, O.J. Simpson had a jury for his criminal trial.

Barbie

I see on the television news that there is a shortage of the Holiday Barbie doll. If you want one you must pay your $22.50 or whatever and expect to get delivery in April. Sure, I'll do that. It's not like you can't get a Barbie, just this particular one. Western Barbie and Baywatch Barbie are plentiful; it's only the Holiday one that you can't get. Notice the name. Not Christmas Barbie, or Hanuka Barbie, or even Atheist Barbie. The Barbie sellers want to include everybody.

This amazes me. I am amazed that there are that many kinds of Barbies, and that anyone would want to collect them. That these dolls with large bosoms, ridiculously long legs, a vacuous smile and plastic hair would become popular leaves me wondering what will happen next. When I have a problem like this, I go to an expert.

Cheryll at the Owl's Nest in Hancock knows a lot of stuff, so I ask her to explain it to me. She tells me that her daughter has many of these things, and wants more. And she tells me that there is a School Teacher Barbie, a Native American, a Dutch, a Black, an English, a Scientist, and many others. There are, she said, ceramic Barbies and Barbies with fine china heads that cost hundreds of dollars. She referred me to the J.C. Penny catalog for more research, but I thought I had enough information.

Then, of course, there is Ken. Barbie needs someone if she is going to procreate. So then we have a Married Barbie, and soon we have Midge and Skipper. Ken and Barbie get equipment so they can go hunting, boating, and stuff like that. And if you buy a special, more virile Ken, he will grow whiskers, but they will wash off, and then grow back as Ken dries. I hear rumors of a Divorced Barbie, same as the others except she has most of Ken's stuff.

People will collect most everything it seems. I am glad I never got into the habit. Of course, that may be because Louise will not let me take my bucksaw and ax collection into the house.

Housework

This housework isn't so tough. Louise has had her leg in a cast, elevated on pillows for about two weeks now, and I am turning into a regular Martha Stewart. I have discovered how to set the timer on the oven, that Saran wrap does not work well as a cover for something heating in the microwave, and that there is a limit to how many crumbs one can allow to accumulate in the bottom of the toaster.

In my search for perfection, I am currently trying to clean the top of the toaster. There is a wide variety of cleaning compounds on Louise's shelf in the kitchen. Some seem to help on the sides of the toaster, but I am a little worried about what will happen to the toast if some of this stuff gets down into the internal workings of the device. Well, I suppose we will find out.

The dog has been spending nights in the basement or the entryway through this violently cold weather. She is happiest outdoors during the day, but is eager to come in about sundown. She comes into the house, checks out everything, and then settles down to picking cockleburs from her hair and putting them into the carpet. We give her about an hour of this, and then put her out into the entry.

Lately this does not seem to be good enough for her. When we are not looking, she gets up on the davenport. We speak to her about this, but she insists, and then I have to carry her out to her nest. The more they get, the more they want. I've got to quit this now, I hear Louise calling me. She must need something.

Mildly Vulgar

A word was used by a friend in my hearing the other day to describe a kid we both knew. I knew instantly what she meant, and I wonder when that word was first used to describe that attitude, that characteristic, of the person being described.

I looked the word up in the dictionary and Webster said it was mildly vulgar, not real hundred-proof vulgar, just mildly so. Its first meaning is a discharge of mucus from the nose, and secondly offensive and impudent. Impudent was the attitude that was being attributed to the topic of our conversation. Somebody was not being respectful enough of elders.

This is not a terminal illness, something that the offensive person will die from, except maybe in a few extreme cases. We all have a tendency to be offensive and impudent once in a while. Granted, it gets a little tiresome if a person acts that way all the time, but people who act this way generally act offensive and impudent only to certain others. They act this way toward people they feel superior to, or people they are nervous around, and sometimes just because they are having a bad day and want to take it out on somebody else. After all, it's safer than hitting someone and it would have to get pretty blame bad before you could get arrested for it.

I am not defending this kind of behavior, though. I would like to have everyone be nice to everyone else. Even if they ask stupid questions, bore you with long, uninteresting stories, constantly repeat themselves, and suggest things for you to do that you have no interest or intention of doing.

Even if you are nice and polite and always say the right thing, I guess you are still entitled to have a few snotty thoughts.

Factoid

Sometime between my 1984 Webster's New World Dictionary, Third College Edition and the 1992 edition of The American Heritage Dictionary, this word was invented. I have seen it used, applied to news releases and political statements, but didn't pay much attention. I have a habit of ignoring things I don't understand. But now a friend sends me the word as defined in the 1992 model.

American Heritage says it means unverified or inaccurate information that is presented as factual, often as a part of a publicity effort. I assume the intent is to mislead, give a wrong idea, probably to suit the person who generated the factoid. The word we use around here for that kind of thing I can't put in this book, but it rhymes with wool spit. So now when somebody tells me about how many and how large a mess of fish they caught I can say "Factoid." Always nice to be able to enlarge one's vocabulary.

The "oid" ending for a word should have given me a hint, I suppose. You hear about humanoid, kind of like human, or tabloid, kind of like a newspaper. But then there is hemorrhoid, and they are like nothing else in this world, and that's a fact.

Weston Kosova in an article *The New Republic* speaks about 34-year-old Jim Nussle, a house member from Iowa as a "Loyal Newtoid". Newt Gingrich has tapped him as the chairman of the 28-member transition team. So you see this new word has a multitude of uses.

> So when you think someone's a liar
> And you are somewhat annoyed,
> But don't want to hurt their feelings,
> Ask "Was that was a real factoid?"
> If their dictionary's older,
> This nice new word can be deployed
> And if they don't know just what it means,
> The friendship won't be destroyed.

I should apologize for the above, but won't, as I am an old person, and have no shame anymore.

Words We Know but Don't Use Much

Louise looked over the first draft of this, and said it wasn't so hot, so unless you have nothing better to do, maybe you will want to skip it.

I heard a guy on the radio the other night talking about euphemisms. About how we are perfectly willing to call a spade a spade most of the time, but when we talk about various bodily functions we get bashful. You all know the words, we just don't use them, except in times of emotional stress, or in a terrible emergency when we cannot take the chance that we might be misunderstood. When we want to make something perfectly clear, we sometimes fall back on those old four-letter, one-syllable words everybody understands.

He talked about the origins of some of the words we use. For example, he said, the word toilet is from a French word for the little cloth placed on a table under a wash basin, to make it less likely to slip around on the table and also to dress up the room a little. Now we use it to describe the whole facility. Thomas Crapper was supposed to have been the inventor of the flush toilet, and that needs no explanation. Another French word that we in America seldom use, but the English have adopted is to call that place we all have to go to sometimes "the loo." This, he said, is a contraction of the word that a polite French person in the old days would holler before they dumped their chamber pot out of the upstairs window onto the street below. I'm glad I didn't live in Paris then, as I am a little slow on my feet.

He spoke of other words, and had figured out the origins of quite a few. I should have taken notes. I suppose in every family we can think of words that were invented, that were used to prevent our children from embarrassing us when we were out in public. In our family the word "Hockey" took on a meaning which bore no relationship to the game, and has caused amusement in our family many times since.

Neckties

This may not be correct. I've been wrong before, but unless I'm badly mistaken, one cannot buy a necktie in Morris, Hancock, Donnelly, Alberta, Chokio or Cyrus. Oh, I suppose in an emergency you could find somebody who would sell you one they had, one of their personal ties, or you may find one at the clothing bank, but no store in the county has ties as a ordinary thing.

OK, you can buy socks and underwear, new shirts and overalls, repairs to your car, tractor or lawn mower, and most anything else mechanical, medical services of most kinds, food for both body and soul, and entertainment, but no neckties. People here have airline tickets to sell you, you can buy stocks, bonds, powerball tickets, livestock of most kinds, massages, whiskey and beer, but no neckties. Even things that are not supposed to be legally sold can be purchased here, I understand. And sometimes people will call you on the phone to offer you new siding for your house, or new windows, or tools of wondrous quality for a small price, and maybe an opportunity to win vast sums of money if you will just send them a check for a few hundred dollars or your credit card number. But they never offer you a necktie.

I still see neckties on men around here, but not as often as before. When I was young, I remember the farmers going into town on Saturday night, wearing their newest overalls and a plaid flannel shirt and the coat from a suit, the pants of which had worn out, and they would have on a necktie. It was a foolish and unnecessary affectation, but they were dressing up, and felt that they had an obligation to suffer.

I am glad that civilization has advanced so far here in this area that the stupid things are not even for sale. Maybe soon they will be seen only in museums, with the swallowtail coats and button shoes.

Education

I see in the papers that teachers are going to have more stringent tests now, and are expected to know how to read and write and even do a little arithmetic. They get three shots at it and if they still can't pass, they will give them another, different test, more suited to their personality, whatever that means.

Maybe I was just lucky, but when I was in school, I'm pretty sure all my teachers were literate. Of course, we didn't have television then, and the radio wasn't that dependable, so if you wanted to find out anything, you just about had to be able to read, or have a friend read it to you.

Then there is this outcome-based education. I understand that if you graduate, you should have obtained certain skills, you should know how to read, write, and do a little figuring. That sounds like a good idea to me. And it will be a lot easier if the teachers can read and write.

I heard a politician talking the other day on television. I believe it was Newt, about making this into a pretty much one-language country, he figures you shouldn't even live here unless you talk English, or I suppose I should say American. That sounds like a good idea to me. I know when we were in Washington, D.C. some time ago it was hard to find a cab driver who could speak my language.

I remember my grandfather, my mother's dad, sitting on a bench in Hancock with his old German neighbor when I was a kid. Neither could speak English, but they seemed to be able to communicate, one in Norse, the other in German. It might have taken a while, and a lot of arm waving was needed, but they could exchange ideas.

So, if this idea is made into law and enforced, we will have to dig up my grandpa and his buddy and ship them back to the old country, as they never did learn the language here.

Nude Dancing

I didn't hear the whole story, just got bits and pieces of it. They were talking on the radio about a community in western Minnesota that was trying to eliminate nude dancing by passing a law, or taxing it, or something. I sincerely hope that it isn't Stevens County.

Now they are going entirely too far. This is something I enjoy, and I see no reason why it should be illegal. Why is it, that in my final years, the powers that be want to deny me one of the few pleasures I have left in life?

I don't do it a lot, but every once in a while, when I am home alone, I close the curtains, get some good music on the radio, and dance naked around the house. I seem to be lighter on my feet, and feel more freedom of movement when I have no clothes on. And it's cooler in summertime, and the cool linoleum feels so good on my feet. I think that the government must have more important things to do, and has no business interfering in my personal pleasure.

Louise just read this, and is pretty sure I have misunderstood the intent of the law that I heard described on the radio. She says she was unaware of my interest in this, but is pretty sure I can dance naked whenever I choose, as long as she isn't home when I do it and I keep the curtains closed.

Freedom to Farm

I hear that Howard Grafenstein is going to tell us what he knows about the new farm bill, and how the changes are going to affect us out here in the hinterland. We are lucky to have Howard. He is able to figure the thing out about as well as anyone, and explain it enough so that most of us can stay out of prison and still make some use of the diminishing advantages of the farm program.

I hear people say that we don't need government involved in agriculture, and we would be better off if they were out of it. That may be, but quit your dreaming. Government has always been, and will always be a partner, and not a silent partner, of the farmer. Any government that has stayed in power in any country for more than a few days has had a food program, because people, for some reason, like to eat, and they would prefer to eat as cheaply as possible.

I may have said this before, but am old and entitled to repeat myself. Anyway, agricultural programs may have started before this, but the first record of one that I am aware of is found in the Bible. You remember Pharaoh had that dream, about the seven skinny cows and the seven fat cows, and Joseph told him what it meant, and Pharaoh made him Secretary of Agriculture. Then he established the Commodity Credit Corporation, and Joseph went around and put those yellow seals on the Egyptian grain bins. Later, the Romans gave free bread to anyone if they were Roman citizens and voted right.

In this country we had the whiskey rebellion, when farmers couldn't get their crops to market, so they made the corn into something more portable, maybe the first value added enterprise. Later the government gave the railroads all that free land, so they would build tracks to haul farmers out here to produce food for a growing country. Then come the Homestead

Act, to make more farms for more farmers to produce more food.

It's not just the Department of Agriculture that is on the farmer's case. We have the EPA and M.P.C.A. wondering about manure and chemicals, the U.S. Army Corp of Engineers, D.N.R., Federal Fish and Wildlife, besides a lot of various other organizations, worrying about our activities and how we affect the soil and water and even the air.

I think we better cooperate and be involved, and accept the fact that we are an important enough minority to the rest of the country so that the government will be in our business forever.

Finishing Sentences

One's mind gets full of stuff as one grows older, and one sometimes has difficulty finding a person's name, or a word that one wants to use. When you are young and nearly empty headed the information is right there, in plain sight, but with us old folks who know actually everything, sometimes have trouble remembering it. It takes time.

I have come to rely on Louise to fill in these gaps in my conversations, and she has acquired the habit of finishing sentences for me on occasion.

Christmas has come, and the family has gathered, and we eat and visit and exchange gifts. It is not often anymore that we are all together, and a lot of five and six part conversations are taking place.

Then, after a heavy meal, and a lull the talking, I started a sentence, about what I have no idea now, anyway I said "I think what I need now is a---" and then one of those lengthy pauses. My daughter, who is young enough to still be a little impatient says "What, then, you need more food, a nap, a bath, a suppository, what then?" She works in the medical field.

Now Louise could have filled in the gap correctly, I am sure, because she is used to me, and has shared most of my experiences with me, and then she has the patience of maturity. So you see I need her to finish my sentences, or else I must speed up my thought processes. This may be impossible.

I have heard of a thing called the "Talking Stick". The Indians used this device to prevent arguments and keep the debate in the councils going along smoothly. When you had the stick, you could talk, and everyone else was obligated to listen. I imagine some rules were necessary as to how it was passed, and how long one could keep talking, but maybe we should have one. Louise could hold one end, and I would hold the other.

Friendship

I was feeling philosophical the other morning and mentioned to Louise that friendship is a lot like Mrs. Spud Carlson's gall stones. She looked at me strangely, so I felt a need to explain.

"When I was young," I told her, "the Carlson family lived where Aldean Luthi lives now. They raised potatoes on a somewhat larger scale than most others in our community did hence the name. Not like people do now, of course, maybe ten or so acres, but that was still a lot of hoeing, picking of potato bugs, and stoop labor harvesting and storing the potatoes in the fall.

But that is beside the point. When my parents would take me along over there, Mrs. Carlson would sometimes give me her gallstones to play with. She had had them removed from where ever gallstones come from some years earlier and she kept them in a fruit jar in her china closet. If one took the jar and rolled it on the table, the stones would get all jumbled up, but then, if you would gently tap the side of the jar, the stones would wiggle around till they all fit together in the shape, I imagine, of Mrs. Carlson's gall bladder, or at least that portion of it that they had occupied.

They had spent a lot of time inside Mrs. Carlson, and were used to each other, and were only comfortable in certain positions. They needed to be surrounded by stones that they were used to and could get along with. They were all shaped differently, but the various differences enabled them to fit together comfortably. Well, maybe not comfortable for Mrs. Carlson, but for them it was OK.

For them, as for us, if somebody bugs you, you have three choices. You can get used to it, or you or them can change, or you can get out of the way.

"Do you see what I mean, Louise?" I asked. "I think I'll go in to the Senior Citizen Center and have a game of cards." She replied.

Well, I thought it made sense.

The Spirit World

I sometimes read the column in the paper that Jeanne Dixon writes, about how the position of the stars is going to affect my life, but I don't plan any of my activities around what she says. That's why it worried me a little when I heard that Nancy Reagan was consulting an astrologer and telling Ronald what to do.

But now I hear that Hillary is trying to get in touch with Eleanor Roosevelt and get a little advice on how to handle the job of First Lady. Well, I wish her lots of luck, and if she makes a good connection, there are quite a few people over there that I would like to talk to.

Herb Tonn told me that my Grandfather had showed him some gold bricks when our old house burned down in 1918. He had them in a trunk that they dragged out of the house when they saw that they couldn't save the building. I'm pretty sure he left them behind when he passed away in 1933. I'd like to ask him where they are. If he didn't bury them too deep, I'd like to dig them up.

I think Eleanor had to take a lot of criticism in her day, and probably would have a few good words for Hillary. I heard that old Franklin used to fool around a little too, but of course people didn't talk about it much then.

I think that they should test the water or maybe the air in Washington, D.C. Everybody that goes there for any length of time seems to go a little nuts. Of course, they are supposed to represent us, and I guess we're a little that way too.

Of course, if you believe everything that gets printed, we don't have to worry about this much longer. Some astrologer says that in 2002, about the 5th of May, all the planets are going to line up in a row, first time it has happened for a long time, and earthquakes are going to destroy civilization. Just before I collect my equity from Harvest States. Well, easy come, easy go.

Bartlett's

I've got to stop being so critical of the twin cities. It is not a complete loss; however, I learned a new word. A guy said that I was a xenophobe, and that was why I didn't care for the big town. I looked it up, means I'm very suspicious of strangers, and I think he is wrong. About average, is all. Maybe he didn't know what it meant, but he sure could pronounce it. I've trouble with words that start with x.

Maybe I have been spending too much of my time looking at all the problems, the inconveniences they pose for the sometime visitor, like myself, and forget completely about the advantages they offer. Try to buy a good bagel in a small town. Bruce, Wisconsin is the only little place I know of that can supply a good, fresh one direct from the bakery, never frozen. All my necessities are available in the small towns, but I must admit that a lot of good stuff, things that add to the quality of life is more easily obtainable in the big city.

For instance many, many years ago I purchased a copy of Bartlett's Quotations. It was not hard bound, but not the typical paperback either. It was quite thick, and somewhat larger in all three dimensions. About the heft of two or three Harlequin Romances (I have seen these things, but have never read one and have no intention of reading one).

It was the perfect size to fit on top of the toilet tank, and the subject matter was such that you could start and stop reading at any place in the book, making it perfect for bathroom reading. The years were hard on the book, the cover was lost, together with several pages both in the front and back, and finally it disappeared completely.

I missed that book, and wanted one to replace it. Then a year or so ago I found one in a bookstore, hardbound, good quality paper, and the 125th anniversary 15th edition. I hesitated when I saw the price, about forty bucks, but I lusted after it, so spent the money.

I discovered that time has passed me by. The 15th edition is full of quotations by the Beatles and other sundry rock stars. Big Bird, Bert and Ernie from Sesame Street have a couple of pages, and I tried to find a quote I half remembered from Tennessee Williams and it was not there.

But now I have new hope. My elder son has come home from the cities and has found, in a second hand bookstore, an 1894 Bartlett, third edition, in good condition. It is a little big for the toilet tank, but if you want to know anything that Homer, Shakespeare or Euripides said, just ask me. I've got to quit trashing Minneapolis; it does have redeeming characteristics. And I am going to start hinting for a mid-range Bartlett's, about half way in between these two.

The Stairway

If you were to go to the second floor in our house, you would notice that a plywood door occupies a good portion of the ceiling in the upstairs hall. And if you were to pull on the short rope hanging down from one end, a stairway would come down enabling you to climb easily into the attic. I call this the Edith S. Sanders Memorial Staircase.

Formerly, access to our attic was through a little square opening in the ceiling. If one wanted to go up there, you had to pull a dresser under the hole, then balance a chair on the dresser and climb up. Or if you had the time, take a ladder upstairs and use that. You had to be a bit nimble to make the trip, and my mother and dad usually sent me to get things from up there, or put something away there. Much more was put up there than was ever taken down again. Once you were in the attic, you would notice a rickety ladder along the side of the chimney leading up to a hole in the roof. This was in case of a chimney fire, so one could crawl out on the roof and put it out. I have no idea how you would do this, but the hole was my grandfather's idea.

Louise's folks spent a lot of time with us, and my mother in law was fascinated by the idea that three generations had stored their junk in this attic, and wanted to go up and look. She had looked at the little square hole, and realized that this was not to be. She was no longer young and agile, and realized her limitations.

It was she that found the ad for this stairway in the Sears catalog, and suggested strongly that she thought I was capable of putting it in. Always the good son in law, I ordered it and installed it.

Now, I am glad that I did. Neither Louise or myself could comfortably get into the attic the old way, even with the stairs it is a little tough. But the odd thing is, we are still putting more things up there than we are taking down.

Places

The Biltmore Estate

A number of years ago Louise and I visited a place at Asheville, North Carolina. Cost us twenty bucks to get in. They partially justified the price by giving us, after the tour, a couple of glasses of the rotten wine that is being made on the farm. The winery had originally been built as a dairy, but they had no luck with the cheese, so ditched the cows and planted grapes.

The house was built when things were cheaper, right before the turn of the century. It was huge, constructed on the order of a French nobleman's homestead, complete with statues, ancient furniture, a dining room with a table forty feet long and perches for parrots at various places around the castle. In the basement were a gymnasium, a swimming pool, and quarters for a small army of servants.

You entered the living quarters by way of a gigantic stone terrace, complete with stone lions and flower pots big as hot tubs, and if you looked behind you, down a three-hundred yard long grass fairway, away from the house, you saw a ruined Greek temple. I believe the guide called it a "Prospect." It had been built that way, in a wrecked condition, to serve as a focus for one's mind, or to serve as a moral lesson, or some other reason rich people have for doing things.

It's funny, what some people work and plan for, and spend big bucks on, some others have just by good fortune.

When the weather gets a little warmer, and I sit on the deck on the south side of our house, I will be able to look south, over the abandoned feedlot at a shed that my father and I moved from the old Fogle place when I was in high school. It has partly fallen down now, so it has exactly the right dilapidated condition one would want, and the aluminum siding reflects the morning sunlight at least as well as the broken marble columns on the Greek temple. While my deck is not nearly as lavish as the Biltmore entry, it does have a planter and a place to sit.

So, we can rest there, and contemplate the old steer shed, and arrive at great philosophical conclusions concerning the meaning of life.

Empty Buildings

The thing that brings this to mind is a conversation I had with a lady the other day. She mentioned a thing she had seen on the Internet, a person wondering what was in the empty buildings one sees as one travels through the country, in small towns, and on the farms.

My experience is not very current as my exploration was performed about 60 years ago, and I suppose the kinds of things in those empty buildings now is vastly different. Right here on the farm there are buildings not used on a daily basis, and I am filling some of them up.

For example, just trying to be helpful, to get the bidding started at an auction yesterday, I bid a dollar on some stuff I couldn't see, and ended up with a table full of computer monitors. They are in a shed here now, together with three bicycles that need repair, an old Buick, the table that the monitors were on, and miscellaneous nuts, bolts, pieces of tools, and mystery things.

I am sure that under the proper conditions, somewhere in this world there is someone that would buy any of the items in that shed, at a flea market or a garage sale. But how does one locate that person?

When I was just a kid, there was a Catholic Church in Hancock, but it had not operated for a number of years. We could get into it through a basement window and we spent a lot of our time in there, when we should have been doing more constructive things. It was interesting and exciting to us, but then everything was exciting at that time in our lives.

There were statues along the walls, made of plaster, and water had leaked in on them so they looked like they had leprosy, with white, scaly patches and an occasional finger or eye missing. One of my friends was Catholic, and he explained to us Protestants who these people were, and about the confessional and the general layout.

The old John Ericson house was standing empty also, and we spent some time in there. It seems that we were in and out of those places for a number of years, but I do not recall anyone ever damaging anything. Whether that was from ethics or fear I do not know. Or maybe fear generates ethics.

North of the schoolhouse in Hancock a block or so was Jacoby's grove. This was another place we could explore, and on the edges of the trees were the backs of the various barns and sheds that had housed chickens, or maybe a team of horses or a cow in earlier years. Most had a hole in the wall or a window by the grove, so we had access. The animals were gone, but things were stored in these buildings, things too good to throw away but not good enough to require much protection. We crept into these places and explored boxes of stuff, and had guilty consciences, but broke very little and stole hardly anything.

Advertising

The thing that got me started on this is a picture a friend sent me. It is of a signboard on Highway #2 east of Grand Forks, heading toward Crookston, Minnesota.

In large letters it says "HUGE REDUCTIONS IN EVERY DEPARTMENT." In a star in one corner in smaller letters it says "Save with Early Detection." and then across the bottom in black, medium-sized letters, it says "Colon, Breast, Skin, Prostate." The logo of the American Cancer Society is in the lower right corner, but so small that the speeding car is likely to miss it.

The sign itself is one of the regular ones that you see on the freeway, telling you how far it is to a town, or a place to eat, sleep or go to the can, so you know it must be a public service ad of some kind. The trouble is, I think they are trying to be cute to the extent they make it a little hard to understand. Do they want you to stop along the freeway and have your prostate checked? Are they offering a cut-rate operation? Now if I was going in for heart or brain surgery I'd take whichever doctor that was handy, but when they are going to work on the important stuff I'm not going to take the cheapest doctor, I'm going to get the best I can possibly afford.

As you may have guessed by now, prostate surgery is a subject I consider quite important, having gone through the process myself. I had promised not to write about it any more, but that is a hard promise to stick with. Ask anyone who has had the experience. It sticks in your mind.

But I meant to talk about advertising. The art of creating a need and then filling that need, and making a buck or so in the process.

A nice name helps sell a product. I remember an old neighbor had a car called a Rockne. It was, I think, a Pontiac, but was made about the time Knute Rockne was fielding winning football teams at Notre Dame. About the same time they named a candy bar after Babe Ruth.

Now, there is a Dodge car called an Aspen. Either a nice tree or a classy town. They wouldn't name a car after Mud Butte, South Dakota. No class. But now I see Mr. and Mrs. Donald Trump selling pizza on television. Is that classy? I am beginning to believe that advertising can sell anything. If done, I won't say correctly, because I don't think that hard, brainwashing selling is ethical, moral or proper. As an example, (and here I'm going to get into trouble) Disney Studios made a cartoon called "The Lion King," a stupid story, foolish, tuneless music, no redeeming social significance, no humor, in fact no anything, and are making millions on it.

The County Fair

I generally enjoy the county fair, and this year was no exception, that is, until the last day. On our first couple of visits to the fair, Louise and I did our usual thing. We would have a hamburger at the VFW and then eat pie and ice cream with the Four-H kids, then look around a little and then settle in a shady place on a bench to watch the people and have a few conversations.

But then Sunday it was my turn to sell popcorn for the Hancock Lions and with the high humidity, I found it was necessary to keep the fire going under the popper to keep the popcorn from getting damp and tough. This raised the temperature in the stand enough to make me pant. Business was not exactly booming. I had forgotten to bring ice, and all the kids wanted snow cones. Then the rain hit, and all I could think of was that my car was parked in the worst possible place, and I imagined it slowly sinking into the mud.

Lightning was flashing and thunder crashing, and I was feeling sorry for myself. To while away the time, I ate a little popcorn, and broke a tooth. I think I swallowed the crown, and now I wonder if I should attempt to look for it.

But, no matter how bad it is around here, it would be worse somewhere else, at another time and place. Here, I am sure I have help available to get my car out of the mud if it is stuck, or at least I will know someone who will give me a ride home. Dentists are available to repair that tooth, and if worst comes to worst, I have plenty of other teeth.

This is still better than shocking barley on a hot day, or spending time in Bosnia, or even the Twin Cities. I have never been to Bosnia, but have tried the other two, and know whereof I speak.

Our Hope for the Future

The discussion around the table of knowledge the other afternoon at the Owls Nest Cafe and Social Club centered on the prospects for the next generation, and we were all agreed that we see problems in their future. The experiences that have made us what we are, are experiences that they will never have. Not that we have done so well, it is just that we felt that we could have done worse.

We were fed differently. Lyle mentioned milk gravy and Spanish rice, two things he will never eat again unless some one holds a gun on him. While he did not like it at the time, he feels that it made him appreciate the things we have now, things that our children take for granted.

My folks had an icebox, and enough ice from a pit in the grove to last until about the fourth of July, from then on you ate what did not rot easily. Oh, we got a kerosene-powered refrigerator later, but that was mainly a bad smell in the house, and was not trustworthy.

Erland pointed out to me some time ago what easy living can do. He had a crow that had been taken from its nest, and he was raising it in a box in his porch. When I stopped to see him one day. (Erland, not the crow), the crow was standing quietly in its cardboard box. It was only partly feathered out and looked relaxed, half asleep. Erland took a dish of milk and a slice of bread, and when the crow saw him coming, it became quite agitated. It would jump up and down, caw loudly, and extend its neck with its beak wide open, waiting for Erland to put in a chunk of the milk soaked bread.

"Now you see," he explained, "how easy living can affect someone. Left to its own devices, no animal is more self sufficient, more independent, or more intelligent than a crow. They have pride in their ability to take care of themselves, under any circumstances. But now, when I have taken away its need to be self reliant, it loses all its pride, and depends wholly on charity. I have my doubts that it can even survive out in the world."

Easy living creeps up on one, it makes one soft. I don't want to give up my remote control for the television, I like power steering in my car, and a furnace that does not have to be fed wood or coal at regular intervals is a wonderful thing.

So I think I will just remain here, laid back in my recliner, and complain that the young folks aren't working up to their potential, and hope for the best.

Medora

Located deep in the heart of the Little Missouri badlands, Medora is a really picturesque place. It has good places to eat and to stay, and the outdoor show in the amphitheater is especially nice now that the escalator saves us old timers the considerable hike up the hill and back to our cars. I hear that they have armrests on the seats now, another improvement.

Not to knock it, maybe I was able to appreciate things more then, but the first time I visited Medora was much more exciting than it is for me now.

It was in the summer of 1948. I had taken a job with the U. S Geological Survey in Dickinson. Eddie Stoekig, who ate at Mrs. Slater's boarding house with me and I decided to hitch hike out to Medora that Sunday in August to the rodeo. This would be new to us, as he was from Milwaukee, Wisconsin and

I from Minnesota. We caught a ride in the back of a truck that Sunday morning and arrived in plenty of time for the festivities.

Medora was a smaller, more primitive place then. The only running water was in the river, and if you wanted electricity, you made it yourself. After the rodeo, having some foresight and not much money, we bought bus tickets back to Dickinson before going to the bar to slake our considerable thirst. The kegs were in a wooden tank with ice cakes, and a pitcher of beer cost thirty-five cents. They were big pitchers. When it's hot, and you are young, even vigorous beer drinking doesn't seem to make one heed nature's call very often. Good conversation and cheap beer kept us interested until close to bus time.

They were pumping up and lighting the gas lamps in the bar when we left, and when we got out into the cooling night air, it became painfully obvious that we needed to relieve ourselves. We were in no shape to handle the long ride back to Dickinson. People were everywhere, precluding the possibility of sneaking off behind a bush, so we headed for the dance hall, situated, if I remember right, about where the tourist information center is now. It seemed to us that they would be bound to have facilities in a place like that.

The top floor was just one big room, so we went down the stairs into the basement. No lights, so we lit matches and wandered from little room to little room, getting more desperate all the time. Finally my friend Eddie said, "I can't take it any more." I agreed. We had tried hard enough to be civilized so we began to empty out against the wall in one of the rooms. Suddenly, we hear a motor start, obviously a power plant of some type, and lights came on all over the basement. We looked behind us, and two ladies were standing in the doorway with two large baskets of food. We were in the kitchen.

I still do not know what one says under these circumstances. At the time, we said nothing, but made unusually good time getting up the stairs and lost in the crowd.

I didn't feel safe until I was back in Dickinson. I am comfortable going back there now, as I am sure no one would recognize me.

Thanksgiving

Louise and I went to our son's in St. Paul for thanksgiving this year. We loaded the car with some lefse and a little chokecherry jelly to have with the turkey, gritted out teeth, and started out to fight the traffic in the metro area the day before the holiday.

The traffic was fierce. I am pretty sure you couldn't have shot across the freeway without hitting at least two cars. The heater in the car decided not to work with any degree of certainty, but in spite of all this I began to notice something pleasant in this mess.

The traffic was moving, as usual about five or ten miles above the speed limit, but most everyone was polite. People would signal lane changes, they would move out of the way of merging traffic, in other words, behave in a polite and civilized manner. I believe this is not typical of crowded conditions.

Then, after our big meal, daughter and I went to get something at a drugstore, I believe it was on about the intersection of Maryland and Dale in St. Paul. A column of cars were waiting for a light to change while we were in the store parking lot, and another car, whose progress was blocked by these cars was attempting to leave. A car backed up, the car behind him backed up some also, giving the guy a place to exit. He acknowledged the accommodation with a wave they waved back and he proceeded on his way. No horns blowing, nobody giving anyone the finger, just sweetness and light. Gives one hope for civilization. I wonder what would have happened if we would have been in Yugoslavia.

Food

Dessert

We don't have the most exciting life here in Hancock. It certainly is nothing like what I see on television, with all that murder, sex and car chases. Maybe it's just as well, though, I seem to have all the excitement I can handle anyway.

I wasn't having any luck playing smear at the Owl's Nest the other day, and figured it was time to go home anyway. I went across the street to the Senior Citizen Center to get Louise, but she was still involved in a card game and the ladies were one short of the six they seem to prefer for seven point smear. I was drafted to fill in.

Lila had made a dessert, and said that it did not turn out like she remembered it. She said the card had "Eva Jean" written on it, so she was sure that was where she had gotten the recipe, but she did not recall that Eva Jean's crust had been that hard. It was pretty firm; I had to pick a piece of mine from the floor after it shattered when I tried to cut it with my fork.

She said that the way she had gotten the recipe, she had taken a couple of days off, some years ago, as she was getting her teeth relined and did not want to appear smooth mouthed in public. She thought she would just stay home, clean closets, and keep out of sight.

The ladies must have missed her down town, because on the second day there was an insistent knock on the door, and as they just continued knocking and would not go away, she finally opened the door while holding one hand over her mouth. It was Eva Jean, Donna, Jan and Betty Z. with dessert and coffee. She was just about forced to let them in, and she said she seems to remember eating some of that dessert, but it couldn't have been as solid as it turned out this time, or she couldn't have handled it.

The Diet

We've tried to lose weight before. You notice I said "we" because I generally got into the diet thing whenever Louise tried it. No more than right, because I needed to lose just as much as she does. We tried some of those food substitutes, like that stuff you drink that comes in a can, we tried the stuff you mix up, Louise went to Weight Watchers and then would cook the same stuff for both of us.

The problem builds slowly. One gets older and you move around less, but food tastes just as good. You can't watch television unless you are chewing on something.

This last round of dieting was my fault. A friend gave me a copy of this diet, said she and her husband used it some time ago. He lost 25 pounds in a week and she lost 17. Sure sounded good to me, so I asked for a copy to take home.

First thing you do is make soup. Chop up a head of cabbage, six onions, a couple of green peppers, some carrots, a little celery, and a package of vegetable soup mix. Boil it until the juice starts to look like soup and it's ready. You can reheat this time after time, and it doesn't get much worse. But the good part is you can have all you want. It is suggested that you fill a Thermos with it and carry it with you, so you can have a snort whenever you are tempted to eat real food. At first it's not so bad, but toward the end of the week you do not look forward to mealtime. I suppose that's the way it helps your self control.

But man cannot live on soup alone. So, the first day you can have all the fruit you want except bananas. Melons are recommended, but failing to find any good ones, we concentrated on apples, grapefruit and a few raisins we found in the freezer.

Day 2, all vegetables. Everything except what might taste good, like beans, corn, or peas. And eat lots of soup. For a treat you can have a baked potato.

Day 3, fruits and vegetables. But no potato and lots of soup.

Day 4, bananas and skimmed milk. Eat 8 bananas and drink a glass of skim milk. And soup.

Day 5, beef and tomatoes. 10 or 12 oz. of beef, lots of tomatoes, and 8 glasses of water. Plus soup.

Day 6, beef and vegetables, and you know what.

Day 7 they recommend brown rice and unsweetened fruit juice, but we had macaroni so that is probably why we look pretty much the same as when we started.

The Miracle

Louise asked me why a jar of pickled herring was on the railing around our deck. I explained to her that it was merely an empty jar that I had been taking out to the garage, and something else had come up, and that was as far as it got. Some days I am easily distracted. She told me that it was not an empty jar, it was a full jar. I went out to get it, to show her that she was wrong, and it turns out she was right. The seal on the jar was still in place, I opened it, tasted it, and it was good.

This railing also held the root of an aloe vera plant that may or may not be dead, a white doorknob, and a large brass faucet. These were things that were on the way to the garbage can in the garage, but required a little more thought about whether on not they should be thrown away. Empty jars with their tight lids are good for holding small parts, the doorknob may work on one bedroom door upstairs, the faucet might be useful and the aloe vera may grow. But where did the herring come from?

I like pickled herring. It is one of the five foods essential to sustain life. They include, as anyone knows, lutefisk, lefse, klub, lingonberries and of course, herring.

When I was young, my folks would buy herring in wooden pails, about two gallons at a time. It was a little harder to eat, as it came with the skin on and had to be separated from the bones. I always tried to get the tail sections, as they had fewer small bones. But we got quite handy at putting one tine of our fork under the skin, pulling it off, and then biting the meat from the center bones. The fine bones you could either spit out, or chew and swallow. Lots of calcium there.

I emptied the miracle jar tonight, and am going to place it out on the railing again, just to see what will happen.

The Pelican

I may have commented on pelicans before, but I am an old person and entitled to repeat myself. They come to our lake in the spring, and float high in the water, like the ships up in Duluth during the grain handlers strike, then by fall they are full of our fish, and settle down in the water about half way.

Louise pointed out to me that in the 14th chapter of Deuteronomy they are called one of the unclean birds that we shouldn't eat, along with buzzards, eagles and most kinds of owls. I'm not sure, but I think that maybe the game wardens frown on this practice also. But then, eating a pelican has never been much of a temptation for me anyway. They say you are what you eat, and the diet of the pelican makes me think that he would taste pretty fishy. Of course, if you were starving and you had no choice, I suppose you might look at it differently.

But there's not much meat on a Pelican, They're mostly feathers and bill. But if one can stand the smell he can Fry them and eat his fill.

Tater Tot Hot Dish

Quite a few years ago, I believe it must have been about the time the stuff was invented, Louise had a spell where she would make tater tot hot dish with considerable regularity. It was good, but like all good things, or most good things anyway, the novelty wore off, it was not exciting anymore, and finally I just plain got sick of it.

I made up my mind that I did not like it, and I think Louise must have agreed with me, because we didn't have it any more.

I had pretty much forgotten about it, put it out of my mind, so to speak. After all, how often does one have to think about tater tot hot dish? Then, yesterday I was in Alexandria at lunch time and went into a cafe to grab a quick meal. A neighbor lady and her mother were there, and I joined them in the booth. I asked what they were having, they said the special, and I said "Same thing" to the waitress. I got a huge pile of tater tot hot dish. It wasn't bad. I decided I would have to quit being so judgmental, and keep a more open mind.

Then, it being Wednesday, we went to Lenten services in the evening, and the young people were serving supper. It was composed of three variations of tater tot, one with snap beans, one with corn, and one with just hamburger. It was good, I had a little of all three kinds, but I think that's going to be enough for a while now.

A Cultural Event

Louise and I missed the Park River, North Dakota lutefisk feed last year, but were not about to make that mistake two years in a row. This is a big deal, so big, in fact that they have two chairpersons and several vice chairpersons just in charge of the melted butter. We had a good excuse last year, we felt we should attend our daughter's wedding, but this year our calendar was clear.

So, we were among the 1335 who partook this fall. Of course, some only had meatballs and such ordinary things, but not me. We shared a table with two Irish ladies, and one of them commented that I seemed to have an uncommon fondness for the fish. This was after my fourth or fifth helping, I believe. She was right, of course, I do like it, and besides, I have heard that it is brain food, and I have been told many times that I need something to help me in that department. Others seem to share this opinion of it's value, as I see in our local paper that they intend to have fish at the DFL bean feed this year. After a few of their number having trouble down in St. Paul, I suppose a little more brain power won't hurt. If the Walleye doesn't work, they should try lutefisk.

Anyway, I made do with only enough bread to soak up the remaining butter and juice, a tiny bit of corn and one meatball, just to find out what they were like. The major part of my meal, then, was this fine, Norwegian codfish, that had died, but had been brought back to life in tanks of lye and bleached nice and white with hydrogen peroxide.

At home, when I feel the need, I have found that a good double handful of the fish can be prepared easily in the microwave in about one minute. It actually takes longer to melt the butter than to cook the fish. Can you imagine those Vikings of old, the amount of pillaging they could have done, if they would have had microwaves in their long boats? They would never even have had to stop and build a fire.

Microwaves

People very seldom rave
'Bout food that's cooked with microwaves.
I know it's easy and it's quick,
And very seldom makes one sick,
'Cause radiation kills the stuff,
The bugs that make you feel so tough.
I heat cold coffee, thaw out meat,
For things like that it works real neat,

But then I tried to cook an egg....

I guess there is a way to do it, but it means you got to read the instructions, and I think that is a sign of weakness.

Reading instructions and asking directions are two things that most men are not real good at. Especially when you get to be my age, we are supposed to know all that stuff by now.

So I shouldn't be surprised when the egg yolk explodes and splatters all over the oven.

August

It's that time of the year now, too late for rhubarb and too early for ripe tomatoes. I can get along without the rhubarb, but really look forward to sinking my teeth into a real Minnesota tomato, as compared to one of those California red baseballs that they try to pass off as tomatoes.

Rhubarb, they tell me, is native to the far north in Russia. It grows best in a cooler climate and does not prosper in the southern part of the United States. It is kind of like Norwegians, it requires a long period of dormancy in cold temperatures if it is going to amount to anything.

My garden this year consists of nothing except four tomato plants, and of course, the rhubarb, which does not count, as it was here before I was born, and will be here long after I am gone. It requires no attention and seems to enjoy being left alone. It is capable of defending itself against weeds, smothering them with its huge leaves, and no insect in its right mind would even consider attacking it. Another similarity to the Norse.

I also enjoy asparagus, but like the challenge of getting it for nothing. Plenty of it grows wild in the road ditches, but unfortunately, by the time it is tall enough to find, it is inedible. This fall, I plan to drive around the county and mark in an old county plat book the locations of some of the better patches where it has gone to seed and is standing, high and proud over the grass along the roads.

Then, next spring, I will be able to drive directly to the best spots and pluck the tender shoots.

Unclassified

Emotions

I've wondered about this for quite a while. People seem to like and actively seek excitement. That is the only justification I can see for things like bungee jumping, roller coasters and other thrill rides, jumping out of airplanes with parachutes, climbing mountains, or square dancing, all that violent kind of stuff.

Louise seems to be acquiring a taste for violence in movies. She likes to watch shows on television where the hero kicks a vast number of villains unconscious, where people are blown through the air and cars race around and crash into things. I suppose this is because life with me lacks excitement. Calm is my middle name.

Arnold, and I am not going to even attempt to spell his last name, is another of her heroes. I saw him interviewed on television the other day, and he said he does quite a few of his own stunts. He must like excitement also.

Johnny Carson, and now Jay Leno and the guy with the gap in his teeth on the other network, (You know I have trouble remembering names) generate excitement in a different way.

They come out in front of the audience, wave their arms, step back and forth a little, maybe make a face, or shake hands with someone in the front row, then say something mildly amusing and the crowd gets hysterical. The audience shouts, whistles, claps and generally behaves like idiots. Why do people do this? Have they been injected with some strange chemical before they are shown to their seats? Are they all drunk? How can so much emotion be generated with so little effort? It's beyond me.

The Unibomber

I have always heard people say that a little knowledge is dangerous. A little stupidity is not the safest thing, either, of course, but I know of no saying about that.

Now they may have caught the guy who has been mailing bombs to people for the last twenty years. Found him in Montana; out on the edge of the mountains living like a hermit with no electricity, not even an outdoor can, in a little shack with his bombs and typewriters.

The poor guy was worried about the environment, and figured he could improve it by blowing up certain people. He was supposed to be a smart guy, had graduated from an Ivy League college, got his doctorate, and then made the mistake of moving to California, to teach at Berkeley, and of course, lost his mind.

I don't get around much, I just make judgements on what I hear and what I read, but I am suspicious of the effect that California weather has on people's minds and morals.

I worry, because now they are talking about taking this guy to California for trial, as the last couple of bombs exploded there. Lawyers will be fighting over the opportunity to defend him, even if he has no money. They are thinking of the six or eight months of television coverage, the book deals, and the business all the publicity will bring in.

We know what has happened to the legal system in California. We have seen this on television more than we needed. So my idea is be forthright about the thing and use the trial as an economic development thing, and have it in a place where economic development is needed. Not here, I don't want all that stuff interfering with my rather relaxed life style, but someplace where all the people could stay, buy food, and make their television and book deals. Right there where they found him would be good, I should think.

Adult Entertainment

The last Reader's Digest had an article about the beauty of the English language, and how it contains so many words. The author estimates about a million, while French has only about seventy five thousand. The reason, the author assumes, is that English does not hesitate to accept words from other languages, while the French try to keep their language pure. This means that English is capable of expressing complicated ideas better than most other languages, and so is gaining popularity all over the world.

But I think we still have a way to go. The Morris City Council had to put together an ordinance to handle what they call "adult entertainment." I gather they don't mean fishing, or bowling or any of those sorts of things. They are thinking about these ladies that dance around, dressed very lightly, while men put money in their underwear. That's the ladies' underwear, not the men's.

That's fine with me, I don't care what they do about that particular thing, I only wish they would think of another name for it, because calling it "adult entertainment" is confusing to me.

I go regularly to the senior citizens centers in Hancock and Morris, and have stopped at others in other towns, and the entertainment in those places is definitely adult, because the people there are all adults, unless you want to be a little unkind and say some are sliding back into their second childhood. But the entertainment for these adults is mostly cards, jig saw puzzles and conversation. No one ever stuffs money in anyone's underwear.

However, today we did manage to stick a dollar bill to the ceiling, and if anyone is interested, I am now in a position to show you how it is done. All it takes is a thumbtack, a quarter for ballast, and a quick flip, which will generally do it.

Comets

A comet is supposed to be visible in the northern sky during the nights for a while now. It is getting big publicity, and will be the third in my lifetime so far. The first I remember was Halley's, the one that is supposed to come every seventy some years. I believe I read somewhere that Mark Twain lived long enough to see it twice, but it was cloudy both times.

I don't suppose I will get another shot at Halley's, but then there was comet Kahotek, if I spelled it right, which no one saw after it was given a big buildup, and now this one with the Japanese name. So possibly tonight, if it doesn't cloud up again, and I remember to look, I may actually see a comet.

The comet experts say this one is made out of dirty ice, I suppose they determined this because of our cold March. They say it is very old, and has been traveling for millions of years from the far reaches of the solar system.

It's not very big, as far as that goes, only about the size of Stevens County if you wadded it up in a ball. It just will look big because the sun is making it evaporate and we see the fog that it is surrounded with. Far be it from me to be critical, but how can they know? I'll bet those astronomers are the same people that were around here a few years ago trying to get us to raise Jerusalem artichokes.

Anyway, it's not that it's something that I really need to see. In fact, I wonder, if I had a big telescope, and located a huge comet coming right at us, something that we couldn't dodge, I wonder what I would do. Not much use telling everybody about it, getting them all upset. People have enough other stuff to worry about.

And what if it hit the Earth while those Russians and that American lady are circling around us in the space station? I would hope that they would get some good pictures of the explosion, even if they wouldn't have anyone to show them to. But then, I suppose they would be worrying about not having anyplace to land, so would forget to use the camera.

So if any of you discover something like this is going to happen, don't tell me about it. If I can't do anything to avoid it, I would just as soon have it be a surprise.

A Variety of Things

I've been picking up quite a bit of new, (to me, at least) information lately. Nothing one really needs to know, but I figure I should write it down anyway. I should warn you, there might be some errors.

The only small flocks of laying hens still in existence are now owned and managed by the weather bureau. The rest are all in those huge chicken penitentiaries, thousands locked up together. The reason for this is that out door chickens are useful in that they will run for the coop when it starts to rain, unless the rain is going to continue for all day. Then they will remain out in the rain, eating bugs and worms, not caring how wet they get. A useful bit of information for weather forecasters.

There are cat fleas and dog fleas. I heard this in an interview with a professor from Cambridge, England who knows about these things. Cat fleas, which are the best performers in flea circuses, prefer a warm, damp environment, while dog fleas prefer it dryer and better ventilated. So, we have more dog fleas, which are harder to train, in houses that have air conditioning. He spoke of a new systemic treatment for fleas. You feed it to the animal, and while it does the beast no harm, the fleas that bite the animal get tiny amounts of this chemical into their system and the lady fleas are no longer capable of having children. They will then soon become extinct.

Then there are the dragonfly and the damselfly. They're either husband and wife, or two different kinds of flies. The jury is still out on this one, but research is being done, and I expect to have an answer shortly.

Sleeping

Meow Meow, our dog, has a favorite place to sleep, now that the snow has left us and the grass in some spots is showing a hint of green. She has been spending enough time in that spot so that she has made a small depression in the lawn that seems to fit the contour of her body. The name, by the way, was given by our granddaughter when she and the dog were both very young. She thought it was a kitten.

But about sleeping. When I was young, I remember rainy afternoons spent sleeping in the hay barn, out of the way of the womenfolk who might find tasks for one to do. My bachelor uncles taught me this, a thing they had learned by bitter experience.

I have my current favorite napping place, my recliner in front of the television set. A baseball game can send me off faster than any sleeping pill. In bed I may toss and turn, in the recliner I snore.

Louise, whose name, I just discovered means "Famous Warrior Maid" naps in the car when I am driving. Whether from a great trust in my driving or from boredom I will not venture to guess.

Then, I know of at least three men, retired, who nap in their pickups. You will find these gentlemen parked by a lake or some other nice spot, head drooping to one side, eyes shut, looking very uncomfortable. They share one other characteristic; they all used to work for the railroad, and are accustomed to getting their extra rest in this manner.

I seem to remember that my mother and her sisters never napped. They were always wide awake and active, I imagine that was part of the reason my uncles and my dad headed for the hay barn when the opportunity arose to catch a few winks.

In our barn, the horse hay was in the north end, the alfalfa in the south end, and as the wild hay was softer, that was the end where naps were taken. One just had to be careful to choose a place that was not right below where the pigeons roosted, and where the hay did not contain prairie needles, and you had solid comfort.

Air Cleaners

I was complaining while in town the other day about having slept wrong, evidently pressure on my upper lip had caused a hair in my mustache to curl and go up my nose, causing an awful itching and tickling. I received no sympathy, only the observation that I had hair going both ways, and when I started trimming, I should get some out of my nose as well as off of my lip. All that, just to filter my air.

A guy told me the other day that back when Henry Ford was making the Model A, you could buy for about fifteen bucks an optional oil bath air filter, but nobody wanted to spend the money. You old folks remember the model A; it had an up draft carburetor that sucked air from close behind the right front wheel. Not even a screen covered the opening, a bird could have flown in and been digested by the motor.

The roads were mostly gravel and dirt, so that poor little four cylinder engine ate nearly as much dirt as it did gasoline and air. No wonder that they needed an overhaul every few miles. It had some other things that I thought were pretty smart though. The choke lever was hooked up so you could also adjust the mixture by turning it. A lever on the steering column adjusted the timing, so you could give the car a tune up while you were driving along.

It's important to have clean air. I suppose that is why we have all that hair inside our noses. It filters out the larger chunks that would otherwise be sucked into our lungs.

But like a lot of good things, nose hair can get out of control, you can accumulate way more than you need. No matter how vigilant I am, mine seems to grow faster than I can cut it, and cutting it is not easy. It is a temptation to put it off, and then people look at me strangely, and then look away, and you know something is wrong, it is hanging out over my upper lip again.

Changing Times

People always come with this old crap about "The good old days." I wonder about their memories. Things were not so hot then. While these complainers may not be able to do some of the things they did then, the fun things, that is just because their own bodies are falling apart, it does not have anything much to do with conditions changing.

The thing that brings this to mind is that we blew a tire the other day. A tire, which had already lasted a lot longer than one would have in the "Old Days." I put on the spare, and went to buy a new tire. When the front tire was removed, it was obvious that the brakes needed new pads. They needed replacement, but I could still stop the car, in fact, outside of a little squeak once in a while, they had worked well. They continued to function, in spite of my failure to pay attention, to do needed maintenance.

Now, when I learned to drive, back right after the flood, we did not have power brakes, or even ordinary hydraulic brakes. When you drove, you always looked for something cheap to run into in an emergency. A sloping ditch bank, a snowdrift or a nice, soft bush could slow one down without doing a lot of damage. It kept you alert, always looking for "Plan B."

Mechanical brakes required considerable strength to apply; they generally threw you to one side or the other, and sometimes did nothing at all. You had to be ready at all times to shift into a lower gear. I am sure that per mile traveled, the death rate was much higher then.

I suppose I could continue on about central heat, air conditioning and hot and cold running water, but you get the idea. For the most part, we have it good now, even if we can't take maximum advantage of it.

Interior Decorating

Louise tells me that I write more than I would need to about my aches and pains and the various problems that advancing age brings. She may be right. Of course, she is younger, and is not yet as aware of these things.

So now I intend to go off in another direction, and speak about a thing that has been bothering me for some time. You see, I travel little, so I can't talk about that. I know no famous people, and have only a tiny interest in sports, outside of playing a little cards, if that would count. So, I have decided to talk a little about some of the things people hang on the walls in their houses.

Crows have a habit of placing shiny stones and bits of metal in their nests, things that do them no good, so maybe it is not so strange that people put useless objects around in their nests. But you would think, as we are rational animals, we would limit ourselves to things that have at least a little usefulness. I own some shotguns of various sizes and some rifles that I use very little if at all, but I justify their presence in the house with the thought that I may wish to shoot something some time. But now I see in an ad for an auction some guns offered for sale that have never been fired and the breech has never been opened. This increases their value, the fact that they are being kept useless. Figure that one out.

I'm somewhat color blind, so when people talk about colors chosen to match this or that, they pretty much leave me behind, so I shall not speak about color, only shape and the use of the objects that we see.

My idea of a well-decorated room would be having useful, practical items hanging on the walls. A hammer and a saw would be nice, right out in plain sight when needed. A pliers and maybe a crescent wrench would be nice too. Some pictures of your kids and relatives might be all right, but don't go overboard on it. How about framing one's marriage license and hanging it up where people could see it. This is a little unique nowadays; not every couple has one of these. We ran across ours some time ago and noticed that one of the witnesses had neglected to sign it. We got her signature as soon as we could, and now are completely legal. I think that this document is more important than any number of pictures of ducks or pheasants. At least to me.

A pile of clean underwear and some socks, right out in the open where you could get at them without digging through drawers, that would be handy. Books and magazines should be handy, pens and pencils, a little dental floss, toenail clippers, all that kind of stuff should be right out where you could find it.

Now, you might say that a house decorated like this would be a little untidy. Well, different strokes for different folks. I think that when you have seen one Hummel or Precious Moment you have seen them all. I am probably in the minority on this, but will not apologize. And you can trip over one of these things as easily as you can the box of junk that I bought at an auction and have not yet finished sorting out the things fit to be hung on the wall from the things to be thrown away.

Coffee

I wonder what the world would be like if coffee had never been invented. I say invented, because even after they discovered it, they had to figure out what to do with it. It could have been chewed, or smoked, or maybe they could have just shoved the beans up one's nose, but they found out how to roast, grind, and boil it, and the rest is history.

Without coffee, we wouldn't have coffee time. Even people who don't drink coffee take coffee breaks; at least the one's who have any sense at all.

Some say that a lot of time is wasted on coffee breaks, but I disagree. Drinking coffee makes one think, and thinking is generally good.

And one sits down when one drinks coffee. As I grow older, sitting down appeals to me more and more. When I have spent time in places where they drink alcoholic beverages, it seemed to me that the people stood up more, and walked around more, and talked a lot louder. And the next day, I had a headache, and coffee doesn't give me a headache. In fact, if I don't get enough coffee, then I get a headache.

When I smoked I associated coffee drinking with having a cigarette, but of course I was a heavy smoker, and associated everything with having a cigarette. When I finally quit smoking, I thought maybe coffee would lose its appeal to me, thought I had to have a smoke with it. But coffee can stand alone.

More and more places are smoke free now, but I am liberated, and can drink my coffee almost anywhere.

Snow and The Dentist

Boy, talk about the theatre of seasons. I mowed our lawn last week and now, this morning, the 29 of April, my younger son has put the snow plow back on the old four wheel drive and is clearing about eight inches of wet, heavy snow from the yard. The record for snowfall here in April, I hear on the radio, was two inches set in 1990 so this eight now gives me the idea that maybe the glaciers are coming and it's time to get out of the way. If I can move fast enough.

They tell me that adversity builds character. I don't know about that, I always thought it was more likely to build clinical depression and bad things generally. But now I'm starting to wonder if maybe when miserable things take place they do have a tendency to make you a little stronger, a little better able to survive.

For example, two of my least favorite things were inflicted on me at the same time the other day, while I was in a position I had put myself into.

I went to the dentist, and while he was cleaning my teeth, scraping away and polishing and telling me the horrors of gum disease and tooth loss, Rush Limbaugh was talking on the radio in the background.

I know that sounds horrible, more than flesh and blood should be expected to bear, but actually one seemed to cancel out the other, and while it was not a pleasant experience, Rush seems to work almost like novocaine on me.

My next appointment is in the morning, and Rush is on in the afternoon, maybe I can borrow a tape from one of the true believers and use that as a sedative.

Chickens

I got a questionnaire from Katie about how I farm, or don't farm, and what it was like when I did farm. She said she is collecting a little information for an agricultural issue of the paper. I haven't filled it out yet, but looking it over made me think about when Louise and I started out here a couple of hundred years ago. I had quit my job with the government and was kind of farming, but I didn't get serious about it until we were married and my parents moved to town.

They talk about the old days as those simpler times, but when I think back, it wasn't so simple. We farrowed hogs, we had some sheep, we raised chickens, had a few ducks and geese, milked cows for a little while, and had a herd of stock cows and four of five horses. Raised three kids, too, but people do that even if they aren't farming. It may have been stupid, but it certainly wasn't a simple life.

Let's just talk about the chickens. As I remember, Louise and I got our chickens from a hatchery in Minneota. They were all, or nearly all lady chickens, because two Japanese guys worked at the hatchery and had this ability to tell the girls from the boys. Girls went into the boxes for shipment, and the little roosters went into a barrel of water to drown. If you wanted roosters, they were free.

When I was young, the folks had chickens, but they were big things that laid only a few eggs in the spring of the year, and then would set on those eggs, and try to hatch them. They laid eggs strictly for procreation, not just for the fun of it. If we wanted to eat an egg, we would have to find a nest and steal a few for ourselves.

We had many kinds of chickens, red ones, white ones, speckled ones, some with feathers on their legs, but they were all large and we got these chickens by just leaving them more or less alone, and pretty soon we would have more chickens.

Then somebody invented the Leghorn. This was a white chicken that would lay eggs just about all year, but it was a little, skinny, nervous chicken, that was prone to pile up in the corners of the chicken house when frightened and smother the one's on the bottom of the pile, and they would pick each other to death when bored. I remember putting red glasses on them, and cutting off part of their beak to make them less murderous, but nothing seemed to help. The hatchery people experimented with chickens, and had different kinds of hybrid chickens, but while they were some what improved, basically they were still Leghorns. Now, most chickens live out their lives in these chicken penitentiaries, but I imagine they become accustomed to it, the ones I have seen seemed happy.

From the time our chickens got feathers until the time they were ready to accept their responsibilities and go into the chicken house and lay eggs, they would run loose in the yard. Then, you had to be careful when you crawled under a piece of machinery to fix it, and you had to wipe your shoes well before you went into the house.

"Catching the pullets" in the fall was kind of like roundup in the old west. These were athletic chickens by this time, the ones that had escaped the raccoons, skunks and weasels, were used to roosting in the highest trees, and capable of out running the fastest dog. Fortunately, they could be out smarted, so we would try to convince them that we did not want them in a certain building, and they would go there. But always, the last few would be coming out of the grove about the time of the first frost.

Expectations

I believe that a lot of the time we think we want something, and work hard to get it, and then we find out that we didn't need it and it's more trouble than it is worth. I remember my Uncle Clarence's apple tree. It must have been some time back in the late thirties he decided he wanted an apple tree on his lawn. Dad and I found out about it when we went in to Hancock one day and saw he had a hole dug south of his house big enough for another basement. Clarence explained that it was for this tree he had purchased, and was wondering if we had a little well rotted sheep manure handy. We did, and later in the week helped him load up a trailer with a batch to cover about a foot of the bottom of his hole. Hancock dirt was not good enough for him, so he added some sand, a little crushed lime rock; some sulfur, mixed it all together and then planted the tree.

No tree under the canopy of heaven ever had more attention than that tree received. It was watered, sprayed, pruned and watched over for years. It would occasionally have a blossom or two, but never any apples. Clarence decided that it was short of iron, and spent most of one summer driving rusty nails into the roots that he had exposed by digging the dirt away. Nothing helped. He had experts look at it, but of course this would do no good, as he ignored their advice. He began to refer to it as his old maid apple tree. Plums, he had heard, must have another plum tree in order to raise more plums, as there are male and female plum trees. He wondered if his tree needed a husband, or a wife, as how do you tell which is which with trees.

Then, finally one spring, it must have been at least fifteen or twenty years after it was planted; the tree was covered with blossoms. By this time Clarence was losing interest in it. Apples by the bushel that fall, more than anyone had any right to expect.

The next spring we came in to Clarence's one Saturday and the tree was gone. "Made such a mess all over the lawn, I cut it down," he said. "Saved most of the wood to smoke fish with."

If you wish to purchase copies of this book, they are, at least for the time being available for $10 plus $.65 sales tax and $2.00 shipping and handling from:
Asgard Publishing,
P.O. box 454, Hancock MN 56244
Phone 320-392-5634